praise for pastor earline j. neal

From the very first time my mother told me about this book, I was excited. I saw the beginning stages of this book in my mother. I lived in the house with my mother and saw first-hand the tenacity and determination that began the journey to greatness. In the small town of Beckley, West Virginia, I saw the forerunner. The person who was not received as a woman minister and the originator of a dance group before they even accepted it in our neck of the woods, so to speak. My mother has always been a person to follow God at all costs, even when others could not see or understand what she was doing. I owe my greatness to my mother, and I look at her life journey and know I have the same abilities. Even when you thought I was not paying attention or learning, I was soaking it all in. So, when I was asked to help edit and proofread this book, I was honored. There were overwhelming and frustrating times, but I pushed through it, as that is what my mother would do. This was a labor of love. I want to bear witness to every reader. This book is a genuine expression of the Greatness that began years ago and written in pages to reveal the Greater One. Thanks for not giving up and trusting God with all your heart. I can do what I do because I followed you as you followed Christ.

SISTER KATHRYN

Everyone has known my mother to be just a dancer and a person who teaches dance. I often wish people knew my mother for being so much more than that. My mother has always been a woman who has looked at things "outside of the box." She has been a dreamer and a person who has always stretched a person's mental and physical potential through her life experiences and with a no-tolerance personality. Often misconstrued, her ability to see things differently has always fascinated me as well. Ultimately, these same qualities molded me and her grandchildren into dreamers and individuals who believe with no doubt that God can use anything or anybody. My family and I learned that in everything that you do, there is a greater purpose. I pray this book will be a guideline to help those who struggle with being different and being confident in their journey toward greatness. I am proud to have a mother who has supported me in all my faults and has guided me through life. Being mentally stimulated to do or feel something, especially to do something creative, is called "Inspiration," but I believe Webster's dictionary must have it wrong. It should be called Earline J. Neal.

SISTER EBONY

There's a lesson in this book for everyone. It will strengthen your life mentally, physically, spiritually, and emotionally. Once you open this book and walk through the journey of these people, you won't put it down until you finish. In so many ways, it will change your life: your mind, spirit, and soul will be renewed. So, enter with a willing mind to learn from one of the best, and don't forget to take notes. Your life is about to be taken to a new dimension and level in God.

SISTER MARCIA

When I think about Mrs. Earline, I think of the times sitting on a playground or in a classroom having down-to-earth discussions concerning many subjects of life. It has blessed me to have these conversations. They allowed me to listen to another person's point of view, feeling no amount of stress when my point of view differed from Mrs. Earline's. My growth as an individual increased with these conversations. As I read the following chapters, I see so much of the conversations we have held. The memories come flowing back like there were discussed yesterday. If this book does not inspire you to find your greatness, I do not know what will. Thank you, Mrs. Earline, for allowing me to be a part of this process and for being my friend.

SISTER VICKIE

ordinary people searching for greatness

ordinary people searching for greatness

PASTOR EARLINE J. NEAL

J MERRILL

J Merrill Publishing, Inc.
434 Hillpine Drive
Columbus, OH 43207
www.JMerrill.pub

Library of Congress Control Number: 2023906306
ISBN-13: 978-1-954414-86-0 (Paperback)
ISBN-13: 978-1-954414-87-7 (Hardback)
ISBN-13: 978-1-954414-88-4 (eBook)

Book Title: Ordinary People Searching for Greatness
Author: Earline Neal

I dedicate this book to my husband and family. My husband, who is always there for me, no matter what. My love for you, Roosevelt, is forever and ever. To my daughters, Kathryn, who took vacation time to help me complete this project, and Ebony, who encouraged me and cooked a few meals along the way. My five beautiful grandchildren, Nataijah, Chandler, Gabriella, Jiyah, and Caleb, who light up my life. To my family, I pray that the writer in you will ignite as you help me ignite the writer/author in me.

To my writing coach, Pastor Jenise, and Prophet Donnell Goss, I love you guys. You pushed hard, but it was all good. Thank you, for we are all writers in the Body of Christ. To all my pastor friends and church buddies: Bishop Frederick Brown and Aiesha Brown, Pastor Cynthia Martin, Pastor Laverne Horton, Donita Brown. Love you, guys!

My focus group is Sister Jean, Marcie Sister Brenda, Elder Jarmin, Pastor Carroll, Sister Kathryn. Y'all challenged my mind so much. Much love to you all.

To Elder Henrietta Davison, who inspired me to write. Author-to-Author, thanks for your inspiration. I miss you so much. My self-care family Eartha, Jean, Brenda, pastor Sancerria, Kathy.

contents

preface

What do I want my readers to learn from reading my book?

Life's Lessons: When I was in school and the teacher said our lesson for today would be diagraming sentences, my heart sank at that very moment. Diagraming was one of the most hated school assignments I had to do. It challenged my mind in a way even God could not help me so…I thought.

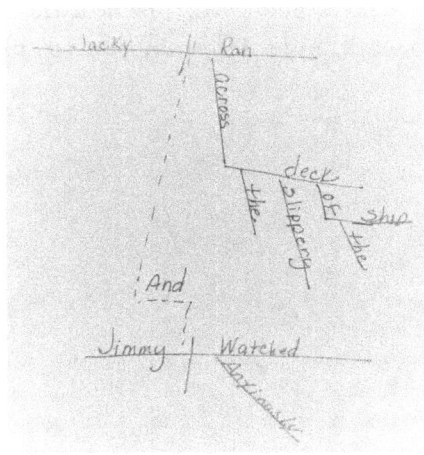

The agony of trying to determine what was what and where it went would put my mind in a tilt. What was the teacher trying to do? I knew that the teacher did not like me. As I looked around the room, I saw the same look in my classmates' eyes. It was as if the whole room was in disarray as well. What was the lesson to be learned in this crazy exercise? How was diagraming supposed to help me at recess? Will this lesson help the cute boy at the next desk finally take notice of me? The answer is no. This lesson was geared to help me in life years down the road, but of course, I could not see this then. So, what did it teach me? I am so glad you asked. Greatness has to have structure to be effective.

1. Everything has structure.

2. There are roads that go in different directions, but necessary to complete the structure.

3. Each stage of life has its own support line.

4. Every support line leads to the end result.

5. Once you learn the process, life becomes easy.

You, as the reader, just as I did, need to know that this search for greatness can be de-mystified with just a little bit of hard work, courage, a mind to work, and a determination to finish.

the journey

EVERYONE WANTS to go on an exciting adventure in life, but few see their own lives as adventurous or exciting. So, we are always looking <u>for</u> others to fill that spot. Have you ever considered how exciting your life is and you have a story to tell? All my life, I have felt that way about my life journey until I realized how exciting and adventurous my life has been and is still becoming.

My destiny had already been assigned, and all I had to do was find the path and walk in it. There was only one dilemma. I had been given a name to uphold, and that name was called GREATNESS. Yes, Earline J. Greatness. Greatness had been wrapped in my DNA before I was born and before I was given my last name. It shined like a neon light all around me. There was my mom and my dad and then there was God's divine assignment to achieve greatness in everything that I did, saw, felt, tasted; every thought, touch, or experience would line up with that greatness that was in my very loins.

Before you were formed in your mother's womb, I knew
you and ordained you to be a prophet to the nations.

JEREMIAH 5:1 (KJV)

1

Until recently, I never thought about researching my name and its meaning. During a casual conversation, I told my daughter about the writing of this book, which confirmed it set my lifelong journey with a specific purpose without realizing the depth of that calling. For example, my first name is Earline, and when translated, it means chieftain or nobleman. My middle name, June, means prophetess or protector of women. Every time my name was spoken, my greatness was being summoned at the same time. The name and the journey, greatness, were intertwined. There was no way to separate the two.

Greatness is wrapped in your DNA before you are born. There is a Mom, a Dad, and then there is God. A person learns to walk, crawl, pull up, roll over, talk, see, observe, hear, touch, and feel. Then there is another level in which one learns to pay attention to voice levels, lights, and noises. These are signs that greatness is evolving within you.

This process does not stop as you grow older, but matures and becomes second nature. As a baby, one is hesitant, but as an adult, one does these same things with little effort. Greatness moves undetected. Each stage of life brings new challenges to overcome, but greatness is always learning and wanting to secretly guide you on a journey in which there is no blueprint. Every adventure is <u>an</u> introduction to a level of faith that will serve you in years to come.

> *Now faith is the substance of things hoped for, the evidence of things not seen. For by it the elders obtained a good report.*

HEBREWS 11:1-2 (KJV)

As you grow, the potential for greatness grows with you. Every setback or every negative encounter drives greatness. Greatness always has a seat at the table and most times occupies your seat waiting for you to mature enough to handle the responsibilities of your life. Seeking greatness is easy, as it makes itself visible and accessible at all times. Greatness knows its place and its assignment. Greatness will push you into position by providing many opportunities for leadership. Many opportunities to dig, seek and strategize for each level as issues come out of the pit of darkness and are overcome as greatness moves you into the marvelous light.

When we are seeking greatness, we must have the right tools. Searching for greatness involves using the right tools. Broken tools could be a hurt heart, old wounds, past failures, unkind words, or someone else's armor. The right tools would be the shield of faith, feet shod with the gospel of peace, a helmet of salvation, and the sword of the spirit. Using someone else's armor will not fit, just as David tried to use Saul's armor. Remember, we have been equipped from birth with what we need to succeed. Greatness has followed us to where we are now in life. Waiting to be embraced and forcefully acknowledged for it guides us into purpose.

Even though in the spirit, the nations were calling me, the journey to greatness was discovering which nation. The mandate for everyone's life is: Go ye into all the world. The world is your sphere of influence, which may be your family, your community, your church, or your social presence. Greatness is defined in your weaknesses and strengths. The premise is to find the greater you.

HOW TO GET GROUNDED SO THAT MY GREATNESS WILL FLOW?

The path to greatness helps you stay rooted and grounded. Grounding is to prevent external forces from taking away things that get to your greatness or deplete you of your efforts. Greatness "grounding" puts me in possession of the things God has promised me on earth. The search for this starts as a child. The fruition of greatness does not take place until I start the journey or path of my greater life. Greatness starts in the imagination. Staying excited throughout this process is half the battle. Greatness is always pushing you. How you respond to the pushing will determine your success or failure.

I press toward the mark for the prize of the high calling of God in Christ Jesus.

PHILIPPIANS 3:14 (KJV)

Greatness is a high calling because it is God's will that you prosper and be in good health (ability to do great things) in Him, and He calls it great according to GENESIS 1. There are no lessor achievers in Christ. All that we need to be is inside each of us. The problem is we do not always accept who we are and how powerful each assignment is. Even our struggles have purpose and lessons to be learned. When we stop feelings of lessor and accept the truth that we are necessary on earth, we are closer to greatness. In every person, there is potential, wisdom, grace, and destiny that has to be released. Greatness demands respect.

Greatness also mimics water. Greatness will carve out a path where there is no waterway or flow, but greatness can also merge itself into another body of water to become larger. Water never stops moving, just as greatness never stops moving.

Greatness and self-respect are like twins. They have a lot of the same characteristics: such as being considerate, honoring the feeling and opinions of others, and loving humankind. On the opposite end of the spectrum, the prosperity of others intimidates neither qualities nor suffocate in the guilt and resentment of the past. Taking care of myself and making responsible choices in what I say and do to allow me to reach my personal goals. Greatness are the qualities coming from within you that explain who you are. Also, greatness can describe a place (territory) that is gained when you honor yourself and your values. Living a life of purpose causes one to step into the true self, which adds to your life and others something that cannot be brought.

8 WAYS TO ACHIEVE GREATNESS:

1. Write the Vision - Habakkuk 2:2-3
2. Turn Every Disadvantage into an Advantage Point - Romans 8:28
3. Develop a Champion/Winner mindset - 1 John 4:4
4. Work Hard - Colossians 3:23-24
5. Master Your Body - Romans 12:1
6. Practice Positive Affirmations/Meditation - John 12:49
7. Build a Winning Team/Know Those That Labor with You - 1 Thessalonians 5:23
8. Live a Life of Service - Galatians 5:14

The Spirit of Greatness housed in humanity is my road map to living a life worthy of my existence. When we stop dreaming or abandon the master's will, the greater life in us dies, leaving us to become pawns in the hands of a society that does not understand or care who we are. What we contribute to the world as a collective body brings more knowledge and understanding of what life really is and how to co-exist with our fellow man without sabotaging their worth. Every gift of greatness is necessary for mankind to be at its best. Wholeness is imperative to sustaining life and life more abundantly. My striving for greatness triggers other's ideas and thoughts. My creativity is to expand what I know and think outside the box of normality. Creativity allows one to enter a supernatural atomic domination that releases a combustible explosion that causes minds, wills, and emotions to be changed and reformed.

1-2 So here's what I want you to do, God helping you: Take your everyday, ordinary life—your sleeping, eating, going to work, and walking-around life—and place it before God as an offering. Embracing what God does for you is the best thing you can do for him. Don't become so well-adjusted to your culture that you fit into it without even thinking. Instead, fix your attention on God. You'll be changed from the inside out. Readily recognize what he wants from you, and quickly respond to it. Unlike the culture around you, always dragging you down to its level of immaturity, God brings the best out of you, develops well-formed maturity in you.

3 I'm speaking to you out of deep gratitude for all that God has given me, and especially as I have responsibilities in relation to you. Living then, as every one of you does, in pure grace, it's important that you not misinterpret yourselves as people who are bringing this goodness to God. No, God brings it all to you. The only accurate way to understand ourselves is by what God is and by what he does for us, not by what we are and what we do for him.

4-6 In this way we are like the various parts of a human body. Each part gets its meaning from the body as a whole, not the other way around. The body we're talking about is Christ's body of chosen people. Each of us finds our meaning and function as a part of his body. But as a chopped-off finger or cut-off toe we wouldn't amount to much, would we? So since we find ourselves fashioned into all these excellently formed and marvelously functioning parts in Christ's body, let's just go ahead and be what we were made to be, without enviously or pridefully comparing ourselves with each other, or trying to be something we aren't.

6-8 If you preach, just preach God's Message, nothing else; if you help, just help, don't take over; if you teach, stick

*to your teaching; if you give encouraging guidance, be
careful that you don't get bossy; if you're put in
charge, don't manipulate; if you're called to give aid
to people in distress, keep your eyes open and be quick
to respond; if you work with the disadvantaged, don't
let yourself get irritated with them or depressed by
them. Keep a smile on your face.*

ROMANS 12: 1-8 (MSG)

Call this a transformation. Greatness transfers us from the natural into the supernatural. The supernatural is a literal place where all things are possible, and nothing can alter or stop this level of progress. We are all working toward progression and not perfection. God knows we are not perfect, but he expects us to progress. Forward movement is the lifeline of greatness. Therefore, I cannot despise movement, no matter how small it appears to be. Even baby steps make progress.

*9-10 So let's not allow ourselves to get fatigued doing good.
At the right time we will harvest a good crop if we
don't give up or quit. Right now, therefore, every time
we get the chance, let us work for the benefit of all,
starting with the people closest to us in the community
of faith.*

GALATIANS 6:9-10 (MSG)

Don't be weary in well-doing for, in due season, you will reap if you faint not. Each step takes us to our appointed destination. Greatness has a launching place and a landing place. In the mind of a child, there are no impossibilities. Everything happens right now. There is no such thing as tomorrow because tomorrow can be 20 minutes later. That's why, as a parent, they may ask you the same question multiple times within an hour. A child's sense of time is so different from an adult's. The consistency that a child has is unwavering and can wear a person down quickly. The reverse can be true as well. Unwavering consistency stems from childhood dreams that follow one into adulthood. I remember my child-like dreams. I always dreamed of the impossible, like helping people, especially those whom everyone has given up on, the deaf community, disadvantaged people, or troublesome children. I have always seen them as successful people. Successful people always see others completing their dreams. I knew then greatness for all people, no matter who they were or what challenges they had; it was possible to succeed.

I can do all things through Christ who strengthens me.

PHILIPPIANS 4:13

Everyone's journey for greatness in either starts as a child. With that childlike faith that pushes us, keeps moving and keeps asking, "Can I do this?" There will be times on the Greatness journey when we will ask ourselves the same questions over and over to make sure we are on the path to success. We must see greatness with the eyes and the heart of a child. There is never a moment of defeat, only the power to accomplish what you see with your heart. Your heartfelt passions present a clear picture of life's journey long before you can actually walk into your designed purpose. There are places you visited long before your feet touched the soil.

When you decide to take the journey to greatness, make forward motion. You cannot look back as this impedes forward motion and halts your life, literally. Forward motion only! There will be times forward motion will seem fast and furious, while other times seemingly at a snail's pace. Then there will be steady as she goes pace while making a forward motion. Snail mail is probably the most challenging but necessary to keep timings balanced. In this phase, there is a lot of control, changes are simple to make. You can think clear thoughts during each phase of this slow grinding process. The snail's pace teaches one patience, determination, and most of all, to trust the God that you serve. Forward motion is the key to progress. Do not let your slow progress cause you to give up on the journey yet. Greater is coming your way.

> *11 I took another walk around the neighborhood and realized that on this earth as it is—The race is not always to the swift, nor the battle to the strong, nor satisfaction to the wise, nor riches to the smart, nor grace to the learned. Sooner or later life hits us all.*
>
> ECCLESIASTICS 9:11 (PARAPHRASE, MSG)

During this fast and furious stage, everything is clicking fast; it seems like everything could go wrong. Your progress stirs a fear that is hard to explain or contain. You are moving at a speed that is not normal to your flesh. Push! Push! Push!

This is a dangerous stage for some. It will trick you into compliance. You will be at ease in Zion and not aware of all the pitfalls that are lurking. The traps that have been set and rabbit holes that look so peaceful. Be mindful of the time; this is when you can easily be rocked to sleep at the wheel and not realize that you are in danger of being shipwrecked.

Because this is not a familiar stage, you never know what's coming. Believe it or not, you can get compliant or fall asleep at the wheel. You get zoned in because of the speed. It's like being rocked when you were a baby. Beware! Take charge of your life and slow things down significantly. Remember, there is always tomorrow. In fact, tomorrow is good. Take your foot off the gas pedal. Taking a line from my grandchildren, "Break it on down, Grandma!"

MY EMPOWERING THOUGHTS FOR BOOK DISCUSSION

The journey of life always begins with a dream. I remember being a young girl and my ability to dream about faraway places and unusual things were always very vivid. The colors were so bright and inviting. The places were very mysterious, yet they could draw me to a place of calmness. In my mind, the dreams were adventurous and took me to unlimited places of travel. My journey in life is to follow just the same path. Start your journey! Let the dreams begin!

when confusion tries to keep you hostage

BELIEVE IT OR NOT, scrambled eggs are tricky to make. Scrambling eggs requires special techniques depending upon the eater's taste and texture preference, such as soft, fluffy, dry scrambled eggs. Different ingredients and heat settings are required for each distinct style of scrambled eggs. The oil the eggs are fried determines how the egg will taste, such as cooking in vegetable oil, butter spray, olive oil, and/or bacon grease. Ultimately, the technique level of the cook will also affect the ultimate outcome of the scrambled eggs. Just like scrambled eggs, greatness has a technique and a flavor.

In being great, there are many unanswered questions that only you can answer. The question remains, what flavor and taste of greatness do you want? What temperature is needed, or does the heat need to be adjusted? What other ingredients are needed to add to the scrambled eggs? Your flavor of greatness is personal that can be chosen from spicy, bland, classy, drama, interactive or any combination of the above preferences. Greatness temperature can be defined as boiling, hot, or medium and relates to one's disposition. Does the heat need to be adjusted to a lower or higher temperature to meet the needs of the person being served? Are there other ingredients needed to make the eggs better?. Those ingredients are collectively known as the body of Christ. No one person can complete the process, as it is a complex yet complementary process. Each unique process of making scrambled eggs needs the other stages to be a finished product. The problem is, if any of your greatness ingredient, flavor, or temperature are missing, the eggs are incomplete.

A great-tasting egg requires a repeat performance. The desire to taste those eggs again will hit at the most peculiar times. Once you become a seasoned cook, you can tell just by tasting what is missing and what needs to be added. Greatness is the same way because it begs for a second or third serving. For greatness to be effective, there must be a desired appetite for it and a repeat performance often. What you desire will not be held hostage.

Greatness lies in the voice of God. When you and I speak, there is limited power. When God speaks, there is a voice of greater in each word. God may speak one word or multiple words depending on the situation. God is all-powerful and all-knowing. Listen for the voice. Pay attention!

Greatness is all around you, waiting to develop when you have a cause. Just like David, greatness screams, "Is there not a cause?" The power of greatness leads you to your purpose because each person has a sphere of influence at the job, at home, at church, at the grocery store, at the doctor's office, or at school. There is no special place that limits the level of influence for greatness to manifest itself. Greatness just is, and it starts with you, no matter the geographical area or demographic confines you may have. Greatness just shows up where you are.

In everyone's search for greatness, there will be times when one may have to change strategies. Sometimes, despite following specific directions to avoid pitfalls that are lurking to sabotage your progression, a negative or undesired result will happen. Be wise enough to know that this does not alter the destination. We can make lost time up at different intervals in life. Stay the course no matter what happens. Everything happens for a reason.

Your desire to succeed does not belong to anybody or anything other than you. Do not let humans, demons, or anything in between convince you otherwise. God's plan is to give you hope and a future. With every step you take, your future looks a little brighter. Be aware of the light around and in you.

Some may think changing course is an act of defeat. When really, it is an act of courage and great confidence. It silently says, "I will not be defeated. No matter what, I will find a way. If it means digging a new well or running through the forest, swimming in a big ocean, or leaping from limb to limb on a tree. I will get to my appointed place with time to spare and endurance to help someone else." Each person who is met on the journey had an impartation to give and vice versa. The purpose of these encounters exchanges information. This information can be advice to avoid pitfalls, encouragement, a fresh course of action never seen, correction, and steps to reach a new level. These encounters are sometimes short-lived or long-term friendships vital to growth. These people that we meet along the way deposit information on how to change our thinking and help us stay on course. This can be positive information to encourage us or warning signs to lead us on the right path. Greatness is multiplying itself by changing our old ways of thinking and getting rid of habits that confine us.

All scripture is God-breathed [given by divine inspiration]
and is profitable for instruction, for conviction [of sin],
for correction [of errors and restoration to obedience],
for training in righteousness [learning how to live in
conformity of God's will, both publicly and privately
—behaving honorably with personal integrity and

*moral courage]; so that the man of God may be
complete and proficient, outfitted and thoroughly
equipped for every good work.*

II TIMOTHY 3:16-17 (AMP)

GREATNESS: THE BREAKFAST OF CHAMPIONS

Everyone understands the benefits of eating a good, healthy breakfast. At one time, Wheaties was the cereal all the champions ate. Their pictures were plastered on many boxes all over the world to encourage people to eat a healthy and hardy breakfast. The first meal of the day would jump start your day and dictate what the rest of your day might behold. Your health was imperative for focus and productivity.

*Then God said, "I've given you every sort of seed-bearing
plant on Earth and every kind of fruit-bearing tree,
given them to you for food.*

GENESIS 1:29 (KJV)

*So, eat your meals heartily, not worrying about what
others say about you—you're eating to God's glory,
after all, not to please them. As a matter of fact, do
everything that way, heartily and freely enjoying
God's glory.*

1 CORINTHIANS 10:31 (MSG)

When I think about greatness being the first meal for our souls, I think of the breakfast of champions. What we should eat at the onset of each day to develop the greatness that lies within us. Scripture tells us about the necessity of food for our health as well. Greatness tastes like an excellent breakfast that satisfies the pallet of the soul. This calms the inner man and lowers stress levels. Greatness fills the hunger pains by staving off that empty filling with hope that attracts the desires of the heart. That same hope keeps you running through all the distractions until the next meal calls (new season). The fuel that greatness provides is enough for you and others that you met on the way.

This is a daily cycle that repeats itself. Each day, the body may require something different, but a consistent refuel is required to maximize the functions of the body entirely.

> *But you—you serve your God and he'll bless your food and your water.*

> EXODUS 23:25 (MSG)

If you really think about the entire process of cooking, it involves how the mind operates and controls the whole body. While at the stove, I am in my world, so to speak. Most of what I cook has already been pre-planned in my head. I know what meats and vegetables I want to use. I know what I wanted the breakfast to taste and look like. I have a created image as a guide when I go through the process. The funny thing about cooking is most of the stores have quick served meals that might work for those in a hurry or a time pinch. However, an excellent breakfast takes a little more time and preparation. Gathering fresh ingredients, cooking, and preparing the food creates a different type of meal. This meal is more satisfying and provides the most fuel that the body needs to make it to the next meal.

This is the same process we need to achieve the level of greatness you desire. There are no shortcuts to produce the best. Step-by-step instructions are necessary for each meal preparation. However, some meals involve more steps than others. Artificial alternatives simulate the same taste and benefits of a freshly prepared meal, but time reveals the truth. The taste of greatness is always different and unique. Duplication or alteration of a home-cooked breakfast looks the same, but the test is the taste. The taste determines whether there will be a repeat of this meal. Breakfast is the most important meal of the day. Over time, that fuel source or lack of fuel will reveal itself as it feeds the mind and, therefore, the actions of the body.

When I start my day, I should start it with the attitude that I am going to be the best me today I might be. When I start my day with a winning attitude, I cannot help but succeed. When I feast on how strong and powerful I am, I increase in those areas. How much wisdom I have being a mom or woman of God with integrity and character are daily doses of food that I must intake.

When I chew on the gifts and talents God has given me, I build greatness from the inside and it manifests itself on the outside. God has given me permission to enhance them each day I live. God's words say I am fearfully and wonderfully made. In Genesis, it says, "When God looked at what he had made, He said it was good." Then He said, "Go and have dominion over everything."

Just chewing on these two truths will strengthen your weakened soul. It will build up your spiritual muscles. Challenge the inner man to perform at its best ability. When I begin my day with thoughts and ideas that pertain to greatness, it pushes me to have a better day because my focus is on achieving a better life for myself. So, every event or encounter that I have that day will be seen through the lens of being the best me I can become. Greatness is powering my steps. My achievement: I am a champion, and nobody wants to fight a winner or a person with a record of being a champion.

Sometimes, when you are enjoying your breakfast, it may take a little push to get that last bite down, but every bit is necessary for maximum strength. Sometimes, in life, we have to push ourselves to allow that last bit of defeat, doubt, and soulish craziness because we will need all the energy to get us to our divine destiny. Call greatness. Do not choke. We have what it takes to get past this choking point. Remember, greatness is the breakfast of champions. So, don't allow a small bit of pain, discouragement, setback, or disappointment to stop you from getting that last bite of courage, strength, and determination to finish the course. Believing in yourself is the beginning of your faith walk of greatness. Get to stepping!

BELIEVE IN YOURSELF

Most people do not believe in themselves. Someone or something other than an inward compulsion has shaped their true worth. Their identity has been lost to the guiles of someone else's ideals, opinion, or desires. We are sometimes in the shadows of others' fantasies of what or who we are to be.

There is always a situation, an event, or disappointment waiting to deter us from believing in who we are and what we can accomplish. Another way to look at this is believing in who God has destined us to be versus what the world is trying to mold us into.

Our belief system is one of the strongest emotions we have. It can cause us to dream big or it can cause us to waddle in the pond of nothingness. It's like an eco-system, but it has to be filtered with wisdom, love, and understanding, or it will not produce the quality of life that our heavenly Father created us to have.

> *I'm speaking to you out of deep gratitude for all that God has given me, and especially as I have responsibilities in relation to you. Living then, as every one of you does, in pure grace, it's important that you not misinterpret yourselves as people who are bringing this goodness to God. No, God brings it all to you. The only accurate way to understand ourselves is by what*

God is and by what he does for us, not by what we are and what we do for him.

ROMANS 12:3

To have faith, I must believe it is through the eye of God given faith that I can see myself in a deeper way or a correct way. I will not think less of myself or be prideful, but I will have the God kind of faith that helps me see who I am and believe that to appreciate that image only. We see we are fearfully and wonderfully made. Genesis said, "God looks at what He had made and said it is good." Then He said, "Go and increase and have dominion." Believe you can do this.

The fall in the garden only happened because Adam and Eve did not believe in what God said they had, which was the power to do and achieve. The snake, the enemy, altered their belief system, which caused a major downfall. Most of our downfalls in life will be stimulated by a lack of belief in who we are. When I believe in myself, I am really loving myself. When I have a love for myself, then I respect myself. When I respect myself, then I appreciate who I am, and this will trigger my belief system to function at its highest level. When we are young, people might say that we have a stubborn spirit which can be confused with self-belief. When we are teenagers, we are said to be defiant. Again, this can be self-belief. When we become adults, we are called arrogant or too uppity. Again, this can be confused with self-belief.

Believing in ourselves can be downplayed in different ways. Do not let anyone steal your thunder. Believe in what God has placed inside of you. Your destiny depends on you knowing who you are and believing in who you are. Believing is to accept something as true or truth. Have faith to feel sure that you are capable of a particular action. Only when you believe in something can you act purposefully. Affirm yourself and accept being confident. Avoid at all costs denial-ism. This word can be better described as a choice to deny truth, a way to avoid an uncomfortable pain or an essentially irrational action that stops validation of an expression or event.

I trust in that value of goodness myself and my ability to fulfill my greatness. This is a type of affirmation that you can speak over yourself daily. This is the daily dose of truth that can propel your greatness. Greatness has already put your name in places that your feet have not touched, waiting for your arrival. The enemy knows you're coming, but there is nothing he can do. The greatness on the inside of you has to be watched from the sideline as you fulfill the plan. God has assigned your greatness to overcome. Do not be afraid of the unknown.

Greatness requires focus. To focus, my vision must not be blurred. My mind is the key. Having the mind of Christ allows me to place a demand on greatness. Greatness is a seed, and seeds carry things locked inside. The only way to deal with greatness is to absolutely embrace it. Accept that a total rebellion or act of war has to take place in your mind when the very thought of not being successful comes knocking. There has to be a shift in thinking.

MY EMPOWERING THOUGHT FOR BOOK CLUB DISCUSSION

As you seek for greatness, your desire to achieve maximum success matters more than your comfort level. The best feeling in the world is to complete an accomplishment or assignment. As I was writing the book, there were many days I wanted to just be comfortable and not push myself. My desire to achieve maximum success kicked in, and the search for greatness overrode my lazy, hazy, and crazy days of comfort. The greatness in you will gently take over the dreariness, and you will sit in the passenger seat and not complain about the dreariness. Your Greatness matters more than your comfort.

listen for the baby to cry

THE POWER of greatness is longing to explode inside your mind, soul, will, and your emotions. Every fiber of your being is screaming increase and for this to occur, and it will take several things to happen. The seed needs to be in fertile ground and water with faith and unwavering trust. The trust must be the inner voice that you hear along with other people that are on the same path to greatness.

> *So, neither the one who plants nor the one who waters is anything but only God who gives the increase.*

1 CORINTHIAN 3:7

The greatness that is inside of you, where does it look for the first drink of water? Just like the plant that has roots. The roots of a plant are always searching for water. It is truly amazing what depths the roots will take to find any source of water to nourish the stalk, the steam, and form new roots. The roots of a plant are powerful. Powerful describes what role the roots play without instruction or guidance; its purpose is to find water at any cost. Therefore, you may see roots break through stones, bricks, glass or anything in the roots' path to finding water. This process never stops unless the plant has completely died. Even if there is a small part of the plant that is still alive, you can snip that part of the plant and replant it. This transferring process brings that plant back to life. So, your search for greatness should never end.

Who or what has the potential to water your dream? Is it a word, a comment, a statement, or maybe just a look, maybe a phrase or a picture? Where is your water when you are thirsty for greater in your life? The sources of water that a plant needs for growth depend upon the type of plant. Some plants need fresh running water, some need very little water, some need to be submerged in water, some need salty water, and others may need the pH level of the water to be acidic or base. The ground is the Word of God and the water is the different people you need on your journey for greatness. The type of water is very important, but also what type of water is needed in each season undergirds the greatness in you. Water is a vital source necessary for a person to grow, but consistently. This is the reason there are different people who impart truths in your life to support greatness. Greatness is looking for water, the Word, and will never stop until its thirst has been satisfied.

Where will that knowledge come from? The knowledge of God is also a parallel to who you are. The Word is hidden inside of you and available at a moment's notice to tackle any untruth.

> *... Jesus cried, saying, If any man thirst, let him come unto me, and drink. He that believeth on me, as the scripture hath said, out of his belly shall flow rivers of living water.*

> JOHN 7:37-38 (KJV)

God's Word is the power source, much like the root of the plant, able to move hindrances in its path. The Word that takes root inside of you searches for water at any cost and will not allow failure. Greatness is there waiting for you to give it what it most desires. To live a successful and prosperous life, the Word has the primary fuel sources you pour inside your heart, mind, will, and emotions. Anything else is a weed trying to choke the root from thriving and killing the plant progress. Protect the water source!

Here is a thought for the giant step for humanity or sanity. What do I need for greatness to grow so the real me can shine through all the doubt and disbelief that has been previously planted from bad seeds or weeds? Experience has taught me that growth happens with little effort, but removing weeds is a very tedious process. Sometimes when you pull a weed, it will regrow. Remember, the purpose of the weed is to kill the plant entirely. Weeds regrow underneath the soil and almost unnoticed. Some weeds disguise themselves and look just like a plant's fresh growth. Often a weed's growth looks like shoot or seedling until it matures and then it becomes clear, as it cannot duplicate the plant's characteristics. The weed will eventually show its true self. It can mimic the plant during infancy, but upon maturity, the weed separates into unique characteristics such as color, texture, density, or smell. Therefore, you must always look for plants and weeds. Remember, they look alike for a while, but time will tell the difference.

My greatness hinges on my ability to constantly find wells of water to continue my success. Here are a few questions to ask myself. Once experience is gained in this area, you can then pass on that knowledge to the rest of humanity and kill the insanity of deciphering between the weed and the plant. The following list will allow you a starting point to help identify the difference.

1. Who are you listening to?
2. Where am I getting my next level of knowledge? Where is it coming from?
3. What is now feeding my interest?
4. What have I learned new today that will shape my tomorrow?
5. What have I encountered today that will lead me and guide me into truth, which is a rare form of greatness?

The person who has your ear has your attention. Your attention is where your focus lies. Anything you pay attention to increases in importance. The Word must take its rightful place as the leader so that greatness can expand in your inner man and manifest outwardly. You can expose yourself to different people to learn new things or ideas. These ideas must line up with the Word of God, but it must be more than what you have heard or know. To go to the next level, you must have an experience with someone or something greater than yourself. So, this is not a person who disagrees with you, but gives you another vantage point of your core beliefs. Like a child, question everything and research the truth. Do not just go with the flow. Go against the flow in your search for greatness. Leave no stone unturned. Every life event has a lesson to be learned, positive or negative. What have our hands touched? Our eyes beheld? What have the portals of my mind encountered? Where have my feet traveled? On what heavenly plane have I landed to usher me into the greatness my soul has stepped into from birth?

A lot of the times, we take the small things in life as just that, a minute event. When searching for greatness, the journey begins at that exact moment that you are born and continues throughout your entire lifetime. Let us explore how that greatness begins from birth. When a woman is in labor, there are many voices talking to you and around you. There seems to be a lot of activity, not to mention the labor pains you are feeling. At this moment in your labor process, there is more to digest that no one has prepared you for. In the back of your mind, you feel a little disappointed. You feel like someone should have told you this was part of the process. When the labor intensifies, the noises appear so much louder. Voices in Your Head, the doctor's directions and the hurried actions of the nurses all seem to intensify. All the activity in the room is focused on this event. As a soon-to-be mom, you are excited and exhausted at the same time. Once the baby is about to be born, there comes a surge of energy out of nowhere in anticipation of the arrival. The instructions are more urgent and the activity in the rooms goes so fast, as if in a blur. Yet, the last bit of your strength is required to birth the baby. The shift occurs supernaturally and without thinking. The strength to push past the exhaustion comes out of nowhere. The focus shifts from how you feel to the task at hand. The moment arrives, and there is a quietness that quickly fills the room. All activity and noises are suppressed, but still occurring. The noise of the feet walking around the room, the heart monitor, preparing the incubator, they all take a backseat in anticipation of the baby arriving. Without instruction or a pre-planned break in focus, everyone in the room is waiting as if on cue for the sound. Everyone is listening for the cry of the baby.

The first sound you want to hear is the baby's cry. The cry lets you know the baby is alive and healthy. The cry releases the tension in the room, as everyone knows all is well. The labor pains are forgotten, the time spent in labor is forgotten, and the extreme effort to arrive at this point is forgotten. The signal has been given. The airways and lungs of the baby are cleared. The cry is the voice of the baby. The voice is small but powerful enough to stop all activity in the room. The voice is faint but still detectable by all. The baby's voice is not words or sentences forming a language, but a single sound. The sound does not have a particular pitch or intensity. Yet, the cry is understood by all as a universal sound that communicates the same meaning to everyone in the room. Greatness has arrived and announced itself as a sound—the cry.

What is the most incredible sound that you hear upon arrival of the baby is a cry. However, the most interesting thing now is how the first sound was created. The doctor uses a pain-induced stimulus to produce the sound. This is a confusing and complex event. Crying usually signals pain or distress. Crying can also signal joy. Yet, the first sign that the baby is alright starts with a pain response. How can this be? You may ask.

We can describe greatness as utterance from your soul. No words or intelligible dialect. Some things that we experience are just painful. There are no words to describe what life brings. The sound inside of us signal everything is alright. I am producing a sound in response to my surrounding stimuli or external environment. A cry that is universally different and still common to all mankind. Just like the baby, a brand-new experience occurred that has never felt before and the sound produced signals a response. Instead, the baby's cry signaled a positive reaction from others in the room. Had not the sound been heard, the atmosphere in the room would have changed. The cry lifted a weight and carried the message of well-being.

Take some serious notes here. Digest what just happened with the cry and the effect it had. As we progress through life, there is always a cry to be heard. The cry can be an external or internal one, but carries significance to others that are waiting and expecting the sound. Greatness has arrived on the scene and has come to the rescue. The cry of every person on the face of the earth is to reach their greater version. The sound of greatness responds from a place on the inside and was not a learned response. It just happened. The signal I am doing fine comes from the inside of each one of us. This is not the normal response to a pain stimulus.

Listen for the baby's cry inside you that allows you to say all is well. This inward shift takes practice, and it is unconventional. The cry response is normal or natural, but it has been thought in the negative sense. However, the sound of crying or weeping is not supposed to signal everything is well. The cry is the constant communication that we send in our prayers and praise. The cry is the confidence that we have in greatness. Confidence is being called to the scene and greatness arrives as a fore-runner, proclaiming everything is fine. Greatness takes the lead and pushes everything else to the side. The Spirit of Greatness is speaking, and all else must bow to it. The cry is carried to the heavens as a prayer, and the answer comes back as a cry for greatness. This process starts at the beginning of life and should be carried throughout adulthood. However, the opposite reaction of worry and fear has become the normal reaction to this emotion.

Right now, the world seems to be in a panic about the Corona Virus. Negative conversation is everywhere. People have put their lives on hold while others are at the other extreme, as if nothing matters or Covid-19 does not exist. Either way, people are out of balance. Having balance creates harmony and helps to maintain a system for greatness to operate. When a mind becomes clutter or altered, this affects the process to make sound decisions, to solve problems, and to diminish creativity.

Always, now, and forever. Listen for the cry of your baby! It lets you know greatness is alive and well and universal to all. Better watch out, "Here comes the cry baby" wailing greatness, greatness, all hail greatness. Everyone is listening for the cry of the baby.

TAG-A-LONGS

There are winners and losers based upon the world system of looking at things. However, there is a group I found most forgotten, the tag-a-long which are you? Searching for greatness will always make you inquisitive. This minor act of wisdom sets you up to be one of the above choices. Remember the title of this book and answer that question. Take a few moments to write your answer and why you feel that way. Now, before we continue any further, let us see where we land. I asked a focus group and their response was close or similar to what I believe everyone wrote. Everyone loves a winner. A winner is a person of excellency and power who displays confidence. Winners know who they are and where they are going. Also, winners pride themselves on their accomplishments and wear it like a badge of honor, which they should. Of course, no one in the focus group wanted to be a loser. Being a loser was just an unimaginable thought. This choice was avoided like the plague. So naturally, no one wants to identify themselves as a loser or an unsuccessful person. The loser was described as a person lacking character or integrity who leeches off people. After the brief, but eye-opening dialogue, I informed the group about the perspective that I was given by the Lord. Simply put, a winner is someone who wins, and a loser is someone who has challenges to overcome. A winner can lose and a loser can win, but a tag along is neither. That is right, tag-a-longs are in a class by themselves. What makes a tag along unique is they are learners of hard things, as their minds are constantly being expanded. Why? Because of the unique perspective they encounter and experience. They do not solely rely on their own knowledge. This thirst for knowledge gives them the great insight into greater things. For them, it is always about the leader until the tag-a-long time to move into the leadership role. The tag-a-long observes and asks questions to the annoyance of others to gain a deeper understanding of what they know or to learn why another perspective might be better than the one they have. All the wisdom and knowledge they have gained beings to divinely perform and they become a sign and a wonder to the world they inhabit. Do not be afraid to become a tag-a-long. Change your position from a winner and a loser and take the position that is most overlooked. According to Isaiah 1:18 (AMP), He asks us to come and reason together with him. Even though something is a fact, sin, there is a way that shall be white as snow (forgotten). Greatness in action. This describes the relationship between God and man that is encouraged and welcomed. God loves a tag-a-long follow me as I follow Christ. The greatness in you will make you a tag-a-long don't worry it is worth the journey.

MY EMPOWERING THOUGHTS FOR BOOK DISCUSSION

The thirst for life is like a well filled with water. Let down your bucket to get a significant amount of water. Once it is drawn up, you can get a drink. There are no more excuses for being thirsty. Seeking Greatness pushes excuses out. Revelation is released, filling your bucket from the well that never runs dry. Those who hunger and thirst after righteousness shall be filled. When you are thirsty, ask God for a drink from a place that causes thirst to cease and life to begin. Are you thirsty?

greatness begins with god

OUR GREATNESS HAS a lot to do with our ability to follow God and catch up to where He is. Many times, our desires for success and the plan we have put in place to get there are far from the planned route God intends us to take. Where is God in your life right now? What is He doing and what is He saying? And are we close enough to Him to hear what He has to say and follow Him?

Most of us have seen the game where a person uses a spoon to carry an egg. The object of this game is to get to a specific destination with the raw egg intact. Accomplishing this feat requires a steady hand, patience, good hand-eye coordination, and a determination to get to the goal line. All the while, there is fun and laughter from the people watching this game. When the egg is dropped, the players must start at the beginning again.

This is how the game of greatness is played, like an egg on a spoon. If you do not have a balance in your life, patience, determination, and courage, the egg of greatness will be dropped.

With all this going for us, my dear, dear friends, stand
your ground. And don't hold back. Throw yourselves
into the work of the Master, confident that nothing
you do for him is a waste of time or effort.

I CORINTHIANS 15:58

It takes strength and courage to master keeping your eyes and hands on the prize. GOD does not always tell us where we are going, so to navigate the ups and downs that occur during the process requires a steady focus on God. Being the best, you can be demanding the winner in you to rise up and excel. You know what is inside, reach for it. Remember, like the egg game which represents your greatness, it takes a love of the game to finish. You cannot allow greatness to fall because starting over is not an option.

This might seem like a lot of hard work, which puts pressure on your nerves and your emotions. The success of the game is steeped in the element of having fun along the way as well. Encouragement from the sideline is good, but it is the uncontrollable laughter over minor mistakes that keep you on the cutting edge of success. The joy of how much you can accomplish if you just stay the course. Once the race is over, there is an excitement to help others stay in the game. This is the most important aspect of the game that people forget. Making it to the finish line is impressive, but leaving a path for others to follow is greater. The advice can only be given if it's an experience that you know what works and what does not. There are a lot of pitfalls and you are doing your best to say, "I've made it. Don't stop. You're almost there!" This is an air of excitement that cannot be contained. Turning around and helping someone else with the same excitement and joy as if they were you trying to get to the finish line.

The excited feeling is the same emotion you experience when you decide it is time to move into your own place. You work for months saving your money, looking for furniture, looking at multiple apartments or houses; the process can be slow but, the joy overrides the in-between stages in the hunting process. The lows are dismissed as the destination is in focus, getting the new place. You have already told everyone what you saw and experienced: pure bliss. The enthusiasm is contagious. You can hardly sleep. You dream about how the place will look once you have everything in place. You see the rug, the coordinating accessories, the pictures hanging on the walls, the lamps and where each knick-knacks and will go. The vision in your head can be seen so vividly. The belief in that dream is put into action by the searching for all the items that you will need to match the vision in your dream. You have already put yourself in a place that you've never seen or been. Everything points to what you have seen. Decisions from this point are made based on how well the item matches the vision.

Just imagine that greatness is a place and you are making plans to move into that place. To move, you must let go of the place you have. The new place has to mean more in order to prompt a change in behavior. For instance, the appeal of the new place outweighs staying where you are now. However, it will take everything you got to complete the move. Every bit of your spare time, finding the right place, your determination to stay focused on the task, your spending halts. This is absolutely necessary, in order to finish the move. The move requires every part of your being to be completely invested. There are so many details and minute tasks to accomplish as well. The change of address card must be done, calls to the utility companies, your identification now has to match the new place. Oh, there is so much to do! How much of myself do I give up on transition to the new home? This is a personal question that only you can answer, but it begs for attention. When you think about greatness as a destination, does it excite you?

Greatness is steeped in the ability to communicate with yourself and trust what you hear. Self- communicate is the power of the voice that lives deep inside your soul that only speaks when untruth presents itself as truth. It is like a filter that stops all contaminated words, emotions, or actions. When angry, bitterness, low self-worth, or a troubled soul takes root, true communication stops the fear of failure dead in its tracks. The truth of the matter is, we are all able to complete the task at hand, step by step, day by day and year by year. Whatever it takes, I can talk my way through the maze of confusion that has blinded my eyes, closed my ears, and chained my hands and feet. Greatness steps up to the plates and speaks in the innermost recess of the mind to stop negativity, which hinders progress.

For as thinketh in his heart, so is he.

PROVERBS 23:7

The Bible tells us that David encouraged himself through troubled times by songs and hymns. Speaking of praise reminded David of where his trust and hoped begun and ended. The same voice of communication speaking with authority to every situation in your life is contrary to the greatness living deep in your soul. The voice confirms Philippians 4:13 and Psalms 139:14. Self-talk requires a complete and unwavering trust in the inner voice. The faith I need to trust comes from my deep desire to hear and trust what I hear. Greatness communicates a higher calling, which will not allow me to be comfortable with mediocrity or familiar with failure. When I trust myself and my God (the inner voice), the divine path will be made known which direction to take.

Greatness will always be challenged. The aim is to frustrate your purpose. Frustration focuses on time and averts your attention from the process that must take place. Advancing to the next level requires a new idea or thought that you have not mastered. Your heart and mind must be clear. The only way to ensure the blockage is to communicate with your inner man what needs to change. Greatness will always birth itself, but it needs you to push.

I press towards the mark for the prize of the high calling of
God in Christ Jesus.

PHILIPPIANS 3:14 (KJV)

Staying positive and on track is my greatness goal. To advance, one must know the enemy and the enemy's tactics. One must know what a challenge looks like. Webster's defines a challenge—to dispute the truth or validity of, to boldly defy.

Our divine capability is under attack. Reach intentionally into the depth of our soul, mind, will, emotions, and intellect, calling forth strength and courage to complete the assignment.

Keep this Book of the Law always on your lips, meditate
on it day and night, so that you may be careful to do
everything written in it. Then, you will be prosperous
and successful. Have I not commanded you? Be strong
and courageous. Do not be afraid; do not be
discouraged, for the Lord your God will be with you
whenever you go.

JOSHUA 1:8-9 (NIV)

To respond to any challenge, first you can access the situation and have a plan of action. Assessment may require you to determine if this is a repeat challenge in a new form. Have I encountered this situation beforehand? Was the response to the question from the position of a winner? Is what you are being challenged with the truth or untruth? You must change your point of view and see things from a different perspective. Choose wisely and humbly as much as possible as you have the mind of Christ. Sometimes doing nothing is an option as the situation will self-correct itself. The difference is knowing when to fight and when to stand still.

WHERE IS GREATNESS AND WHERE DO I LOOK?

Many people ask themselves this question time after time. Every person knows there is more than what meets the natural eye or ear. For some, it is elusive as they just cannot obtain greatness even though the desire is there. Then the question becomes, how do I tap into that greatness? The answer to this question can be found in the Bible.

> *What no eye has seen, what no ear has heard, and what no human mind has conceived the things God has prepared for those who love Him- these are the things God has revealed to us by His Spirit.*

> I CORINTHIANS 2:9-10

Trust what God has imparted to you; those deep-seated desires only you know. Those ideas, dreams, and visions that are constantly being played on the reels of your mind and heart. Let me make this point very clear. Focus on the positive side of your life and not the doom and gloom experiences. The great things in your life that make you feel as if you are on top of the world and do not care who knows it part of your life. There is a divine principle that God will not let you fail because that would be an impossibility. Your future is always greater than your past. Greatness demands that empower the inner seeker, the Holy Spirit. The inner seeker for greatness leads and guides us unto all truth, according to John 16:13 (KJV). The desire to obtain greatness correlates directly to the relationship we have with the Holy Spirit.

But the Comforter (Counselor, Helper, Intercessor,
Advocate, Strengthener, Standby), the Holy Spirit,
Whom the Father will send in My name [in My place,
to represent Me and act on My behalf], He will teach
you all things. And He will cause you to recall (will
remind you of, bring to your remembrance)
everything I have told you.
Peace I leave with you, My [own] peace I now give and
bequeath to you. Not as the world gives do I give to
you. Do not let your hearts be troubled, neither let it
be afraid. [Stop allowing yourselves to be agitated and
disturbed; and do not permit yourselves to be fearful
and intimidated and cowardly and unsettled.]

JOHN 14: 26-27

The Holy Spirit gives us insight that helps us more effectively work out the calling or plan for our lives and those around us. The Father reveals those hidden mysteries to the people of God. This is our inheritance, as the prior verse tells us the Holy Spirit's advice is bequeath or left to us in a will which is a legal document. This means guidance is a legal right and we have the authority to possess those things left by the Father. This right was prepared in heaven and it is a SPIRITUAL LAW that dictates earthly events.

Therefore, anything that does not line up with the word of God, I have the authority to redirect it spiritually until it manifests in the natural world. Those divine directions belong to me and I possess them. There are no delays, setbacks, hindrances, no substitutes or obstacles that cannot be overcome. The truth of God's plan is known by the Holy Spirit, and I have direct access to those blueprints legally. Tell yourself in the mirror daily:

I decree and declare that I have an innovative kingdom mentality that opens a new way of thinking and being. Nothing in and of this world can stop what legally belongs to me. The Holy Spirit hears the will and voice of God. As an advisor to me, the Holy Spirit reveals and teaches me what he hears in the throne room of God. I have been willed with those plans and directions. I open my heart to hear and receive what the Father says. I no longer am in the position of not knowing what to do. The Holy Spirit guides me with divine directions, which are necessary. Daily, I seek to hear and take action on what I have received from the Holy Spirit. I rehearse and meditate on those plans as the Holy Spirit brings to my remembrance all things that pertain to God. I shall not stumble or fail. My mind, will, emotions, heart, and intellect are alert and ready to move, which causes me to be successful and prosperous in all that I do. Divine authority belongs to me in Jesus's name. Amen!

Greatness always has doors of opportunities. The challenge is to muster the courage to open the door. When we are unsure of what we cannot see, touch, feel or hear, we will be reluctant about opening these doors of opportunity. Fear of the unknown always stifles progress.

> *Be strong and courageous, because you will lead these people to inherit the land I swore to their ancestors to give them. Be strong and very courageous. Be careful to obey all the law my servant Moses gave you do not turn from it to the right or to the left, that you may be successful wherever you go. Keep this Book of the Law always on your lips, meditate on it day and night, so that you may be careful to do everything written in it. Then you will be prosperous and successful. Have I not commanded you? Be strong and courageous. Do not be afraid, do not be discouraged, for the Lord your God will be with you, whenever you go.*

JOSHUA 1:6-9 (NIV)

To exercise these principles, I must do so without making excuses. I cannot negotiate with my flesh, mind, or my will. I must override any negative force that tries to stop greatness from emerging from within myself. One of the greatest setbacks in anyone's life is missed opportunities. When this happens, I ask myself, "How do I stop the bleeding?" In real life, greatness involves locating pressure points. I desire to know where they are and how to apply the needed pressure on them correctly to eliminate giving up in life.

PRESSURE POINTS TO PONDER

1. Knowledge of who you are according to the Word of God.
2. Know your weaknesses, as well as your strengths.
3. Know what triggers doubt and what makes you want to quit.
4. Improve your relationship with others.
5. Work on separating your wants and desires.

The pressure points are a starting point to lead you to your greatness. The first step is searching the scriptures to find out who you are. This requires meditation and allowing the Holy Spirit to direct you to what you need. There are many Bible characters to draw direction on success and pitfalls they encountered on their journey. When you research the characters you love or dislike, place yourself in the story. Ask the Holy Spirit to reveal to you how your life you parallel those characters, flaws and all. Until you humbly place yourself in those situations, you can never know all your strengths and weaknesses. The characters in the Bible were real people that did not always follow God's plan but were all accounted for, just like your life is also pre-planned. In the Bible, Jesus always related to others, no matter their walk of life. This is very important as you will have people from different economic, social, and belief systems than yours. Jesus teaches us to be all things to all people. Learn and seek flexibility in your relationships to reach others. The last point, look for ways to separate your needs and wants. This will require much direction from the Holy Spirit and an open mind. Sometimes, what we want is not needed to fulfill our greatness, and sometimes, our desires may cloud our judgment. Ask the Holy Spirit to direct your wants and desire to the will of God. This is the hardest part, but yields the most effective way to achieve your greatness.

MY EMPOWERING THOUGHTS FOR BOOK CLUB DISCUSSIONS

Truth is a rare form of greatness. What do you expect from God? Sometimes, we work too hard to get to external validation. The truth of the matter is greatness comes from God who says, "I am the truth, the way and the life. No man cometh unto the Father, except by Me," according to John 14:6. My greatness is to connect to my relationship with the Father. He said, "I am the Alpha and Omega, the Beginning and the End of every living thing." Another way to think about this is God is my anchor. So, I do not drift out to sea, where nothingness is waiting to sabotage my hopes and vision.

checkpoints for success

YOUR LIFE HAS PURPOSE. God's plan for you is unchanged. Every day I listen for the voice of God and what it says to me. I have trained myself to set aside time each day and just wait on the Lord. Most of the time, it occurs in the morning, but that is my preference and routine. When I hear what God has to say, it is always new and exciting thoughts. I call these times my "when I hear God's voice: Empowering Thoughts." This is one that I want to share and encourage you to ponder in your alone time with God as well. Keep a journal to write. As you go through your day, allow your mind to think about what you heard.

Empowering Thought

Dream, Dream, Dream
Your Voice Will Always Matter
You Were Born into Greatness
Seek for Greatness with Everything That You Have
You Will Impact the World!

Greatness will always challenge the champion in you and me. When the unseen lion in us roars for exposures, the lion roars to be seen, felt, and heard. Champions take quality time to prepare for the fight. The fight appears effortless and taken lightly by most observers. Most people who watch a fight do not realize the time and effort that is spent to prepare for the actual fight. Once the fight begins, the motions are second nature and require little or no thoughts, as the repetition done during practice kicks into high gear. Hours, days, weeks, and years of doing the same thing again and again are seen during the fight, but the amount of dedication and focus would astonish the normal person. To be the best, you must progress beyond the normal way of doing things. This process is a mindset that increases with each victory and eliminates weakness with each defeat. In the final fight, the lion emerges and roars as the champion.

For most Christians, the roar of the lion needs development. The ability to stand and say: Yes, I am a champion. My spirit tells me so. I heard from God what was needed to find the champion in me to win. The answer is pray, plan, and produce. Those three things are needed on the practice field of life's game plan to win.

God reminded me of words starting with the aftermath/residue of life. He said a clean-up was needed, but not until everything was completed. Do not regret now. God showed me that prayer was needed. The prayer is very specific and should center on repentance. After repentance has been offered in prayer, then praise should be given for his ability to restore. God also allowed me to see that people are not in charge. He is, and the focus must be put back on Him. Last, the Lord showed me divine guidance was needed to know where and when we should go. What Is required for future success is 20/20 vision. God will lead His people to safety, but needs anointed people who can see clearly to destroy yokes and lift burdens. This vision will usher in wholeness, prosperity, peace, wisdom. God is making a download in you for divine leadership and spiritual government.

Greatness cannot be achieved by having a good feeling. I do not need people to tell me what feels good. If push comes to shove, I can make myself feel good. What I need is for someone to tell me the truth. Greatness takes determination, strength, and courage. I need a mental fortitude that goes beyond felling. When I succumb to a feeling, it weakens my resolve and diminishes my abilities to strive for greatness and the best person who I can be.

Feelings come and go. Feelings are sometimes up and sometimes down. So, emotions can play tricks on a person. I need events or situations requiring another person to stir me up or migrate me into a new avenue of truth. I need truth to ring like a liberty bell in a way that is loud, precise, and clear.

> *And you shall know the truth and the truth shall make*
> *you free.*

> JOHN 8:32 (KJV)

The truth is the only thing that will produce greatness. We can describe truth as a mental capacity to perceive words or actions in a deeper way. In the Bible, Jesus did not back off from telling people the truth. The most important aspect of his ministry was to give the truth in parables. Parables was a way to give unadulterated truth, but in a way that others would readily receive and ponder the meaning of His words. Effective truth reaches heart and prompts a change from a particular course of action or starts a new one. In contrast, greatness stalls when it cannot receive truth. When was the last time you failed to receive a truth about yourself?

> *In this way we are like the various parts of a human body.*
> *Each part gets its meaning from the body a whole, not*
> *the other way around.*

> ROMANS 12: 4-5 (MSG)

The body we are talking about is Christ's body of chosen people. Each of us finds our meaning and function as part of His body. With a chopped-off finger or cut-off toe, we would not amount too much, would we? We find ourselves fashioned into all these extremely formed and marvelously functioning parts in Christ's body.

Without an accurate measure of yourself and what you can achieve, this steers you in the wrong direction. Greatness becomes stuck where you are and cannot move without a change. Greatness requires a challenge based upon truth and honesty to operate at a peak level. You should look for ways to push yourself that are unconventional. Productivity requires a different mindset to navigate the winding roads of greatness that lie ahead.

When we start our journey called life, no one tells us with clarity what the future will hold. So, we approach life like an untrained driver full speed ahead. Whatever seems to hold us back or get in our way is quickly dismantled with screaming, angry, and throwing tantrum, which leaves us highly exhausted. The energy expelled could have been used to explore and define your dreams and expectations. I caution you because the lack of experience or proper guidance hinders future results.

These can be better defined as checkpoints. Throughout life, no matter how old or young, we all need checkpoints to stay on the God-given path to greatness. When we plow past the checkpoints' dangers lurk, we miss the road signs and get off course, which takes time to retract or redirect paths already traveled. The real danger in getting back on course is that it may take weeks, months, or years to realize we are going in the wrong direction. These redirects can be shortened by moments of reflection. The value of redirects can be time savers if used correctly by allowing us the opportunity to strategize with control.

*For which of you, intending to build a tower sitteth not
down first, and counteth the cost, whether he have
sufficient to finish it? Lest haply, after he hath laid the
foundation, and is not able to finish it, all the behold
it begin to mock him. Saying, this man began to build,
and was not able to finish.*

LUKE 14:28-30

These seasons of your life require planning, consulting with others, looking into finances, and altering previous plans to finish the task. These are short-term goals and require daily checking to gauge where you are and which direction is needed when unforeseen events occur. That is when prayer and communication with God are your sword and shield. If you are not careful, you can grow weary in doing good, if you lose your focus on achieving greatness.

THE PURPOSE OF CHECKPOINTS

God has delegated your authority to execute greatness. Along with that authority comes the ability to:

1. Focus on what you already know.
2. Interrogate yourself with questions.
3. Be clear on the next steps.
4. Use past experiences and new ones.
5. Pick your next move smartly.

Greatness requires diligence in everything you do. Each accomplishment is a stepping-stone to a new level to explore. This process I call peeling the orange. The orange is peeled one layer at a time to get the goodness waiting on the inside. Greatness operates the same way. Victory looks good on you. Remember, each victory releases energy that motivates you to get to the next level.

Checkpoint! Every part of the orange can be useful. The orange peel was the labor, but it can be used for other things. In life there may be some things that you labor over, but waste nothing such as time, finances, fasting, prayer and/or thanksgiving. Use the natural and supernatural. Both are useful and necessary. Checkpoint! Do not exhaust the natural, then consult the supernatural. Learn to operate in reverse. Call upon the supernatural to direct the natural things. This change in thinking will make up lost time and allow accuracy in future choices. Working smarter, not harder. God is not obligated to provide provision for what He has not given purpose to. Consulting God first allows God to provide sweat with fewer provisions needed along the way.

In your search for greatness, you have to self-talk. Silence is not an option or a consideration. Each individual has to learn how to talk his or her way through the maze of destruction, which has traps set to undermine your progress. Sometimes the traps can set you back or make you totally want to throw in the towel. However, learning how to self-talk is an act of confidence. It is one of the first lines of defense. There will be many voices that you hear in your head, around you in your sphere of influence family, friends with their opinion and so on. Your voice and the voice of God will become the same. The two must merge into one just as Jesus and the Father became one.

> *I am able to do nothing from Myself [independently, of My own accord-but only as I am taught by God and as I get his Orders]. Even as I hear, I judge [I decide as I am bidden to decide. As the voice comes to Me, so I give a decision], and My judgment is right (just, righteous), because I do not seek or consult My own will [I have no desire to do what is pleasing to Myself, My own aim, My own purpose] but only the will and pleasure of the Father Who sent Me.*

JOHN 5:30 (AMP)

Our knowledge of scripture will help. There should be a knowledge of life rules, cultural rules, spiritual government, etiquette, and so on. The knowledge needed involves spiritual laws and natural laws. Having these will enhance your ability to succeed.

One of the great mysteries of life is everything God created has life. Each life form has a voice that constantly communicates with someone or something. That same voice speaks verbally or non-verbally. Everything around us speaks its own language. The most magnificent thing is that man has the authority, as given in Genesis, to direct all the other voices and things in the environment. Man's voice carries the authority given from God, even though everything that contains life can speak. So, how we use the authority is of utmost importance. What we say, how we say it, when we say it, and why we say it must connect to a divine purpose to continue life.

The greatness of God is in me. When God created male and female, He only had greatness on His mind. We are created in the image and likeness of God. The image of His likeness is greatness. Great is the Lord! When we think about greatness, what does that mean to you and me? Who God has created us to be is drenched in a sea of greatness. When we look at the grains of sand on the beach and how vast they are, or consider the sea and the depths of the water as far as the eye can see, we are in amazement. All of creation is an express of God's greatness.

As a creation of God's handiwork, we forget we were made in His image and likeness. Meaning that we all can do the same thing. God created the world for mankind to have a visual or sensory image to see His greatness. Therefore, we are visionaries drawing from the spirit. We under-utilize what was given to us freely—who you are in Christ and the Christ that is in you. Just as we see things in the natural, the spirit man sees greatness much the same way. Greatness must be manifested in the natural world as well, but starts on the inside. To get this process started, we must visualize it first, then speak it into existence, touch it with own very-being. The inner man must use every part of its being to produce greatness. The whole body has a part to play. Allow your voice to occupy space and time and call forth greatness. Until you can experience this with your soul, mind, body, will, emotions, and intellect, you will always fall short of how great you really are.

THE ROADMAP TO GREATNESS:

1. We are fearfully and wonderfully made in God's image and likeness.
2. To get past the choking point, you must learn to breathe.
3. To catch the vision of God's purpose and God's people is my goal.
4. Greatness is tied to the movement, and when God spoke, things fell into their place.
5. God's Word moves everything.
6. God's Word makes things come alive.

Great people have a voice.
Great people speak the truth.
Great people are full of wisdom.
Great people speak with spiritual authority and change the direction of everything.
Great people bring life to dead things.
Great people are reliable.
Great people are loyal.
Great people walk strong in integrity and character.
Great people are dreamers.
Great people are compassionate.
Great people operate in truth only.

Great people see the greatness in others.
Great people are willing to mentor others.
Great people value developing greatness.

My desire for total greatness hinge on my ability to follow God. Sometimes, it is not the ability to follow, but the ability to catch up to where God is. Many times, our desire for success and the plans we have put into place to get there are far from the plan of God. God has a route He wants us to take us. Where is God in your life right now? What is He doing and what is He saying? Are we close enough to Him to hear what He has to say or follow His directions? Can we see Him point us to the correct path or direction that we need?

You are here. God is there. If we want to get from here to there, we must follow God or better yet, catch up to where He is. Run! Time is of the essence. Greatness is always on God's calendar. God shuts everything down around us for us to tap into his plan and follow the path He has designed for just us. What is your route to greatness? Do you know? Do you remember the children of Israel who took more time than necessary to get to their greatness? This is called "our place of promises."

The other thing that helps in your greatness route is a spirit of thanksgiving and praise. Taking the time to show God your appreciation by praising Him for His help. This also works in your day-to-day sphere of influence. Do not forget to thank the people who have imparted greatness in your life. This ensures humility as no one person creates greatness in and of themselves. Greatness starts on the inside and, to increase it, requires impartations from others or events that occur in your life. Forgetting to have a spirit of thanksgiving and praise keeps you in a holding pattern, much like a plane that cannot land. You are circling around your destination, but stuck there and not able to reach the actual destination on the ground. There is so much time that can be lost here. The sad thing is this portion of your life is completely under your control. Once you start the process of self-talk and see results, do not forget to turn around and thank God and the people who have been instrumental in your greatness. This may seem like an obvious position to take, but few people take the time to do it. Like a mother who does so many things behind the scenes and rarely receives a thank-you for the small things that keep the house running. This slight gesture can hinder your progress. Take control and get your greatness out of a holding pattern.

MY EMPOWERING THOUGHTS FOR BOOK CLUB DISCUSSION

Your vision becomes clear the higher you go. There are many people who are afraid of heights. The higher up they go, the more anxious they become. They are fearful and they can become frozen in that space and time. They sweat and are very nauseous. They will tell you it is the worst feeling ever. I do not downplay this at all. We all have been there. The higher up you go, things become clearer. Once you realize how far you are from the ground, every rock or mountain seems bigger than life. Things are now clearer than they have ever been. Going higher in life can be scary, but the vision from that place is so much sharper. Use your faith to help you climb. Check your vision!

starting the journey requires work and dedication

SEEKERS FIND JOY SEARCHING. When you have unknown spiritual gifts, the joy of it is searching for the invisible; the unseen that lies in the unearthed mysteries of knowledge. It is like finding a diamond in the middle of a piece of coal. Searching in an unusual place where this type of gemstone would probably never be, but the nature of the seeker is all things are possible to them that believe according to Mark 9:23. So, seekers go beyond the normal or, let's say, beyond the natural and they tap into the supernatural. Much like a kid who does not mind playing in the dirt or walking in the rain. The adventure and what happens along the way intrigue a seeker to go deeper, expecting something will be there. A positive attitude brings joy to their heart and compels them into deeper levels of great possibilities. When we seek greatness, this happens: it demands that we always go beyond what the natural man can perceive. Searching allows us the joy of finding the unpredictable corners of life, the uncommon field or place to find treasures.

In taking those baby steps, give praise to each milestone. What this does is put you in a position to achieve more and more. Your appetite for success or excellence has now been programmed, so you have a hunger and a thirst for more. This is a journey that never plateaus but always looks toward the next level. It is like when a baby takes those first steps. It is not the stepping that triggers you to do it again, but it is the praise and the loving hugs that the baby receives from the arms of an excited mother. Constant reassurance from the voice of the mother excites the baby and making more steps becomes motivational. Seekers of greatness know how to celebrate their own accomplishments, great or small. The only difference is all this excitement and praise should be followed by a time and a season of praise to ignite the joy of your salvation. Then you can sing that age-old hymnal.

> *He touched me, Oh He touched me,*
> *And Oh the joy that floods my soul!*
> *Something happened and now I know,*
> *He touched me and made me whole.*

That something in this hymn is the touch given to you—the hand of greatness. According to James 1:2-4:

> *Consider it nothing but you, my brothers and sisters,*
> *whenever you fall into various trials. Be assured that*
> *the testing of your faith [through experience] produce*
> *endurance [leading to spiritual maturity and inner*
> *peace]. And let endurance have its perfect result and*
> *do a thorough work so that you make be perfect and*
> *completely developed [in your faith], lacking in*
> *nothing.*

The best medicine to take that heals quickly and completes for the inner man is joy. When we learn to find the joy in what we do instead of dread, it transforms our lives. Joy stirs up hope, and hope makes us not ashamed of what we have achieved. Therefore, it is good to not downplay the results. Rejoice, no matter what the outcome or ultimate result triggers your well-being. When we become seekers of greater things for ourselves, our family, and life, we develop our well-being. Our desires to achieve more speeds up with a vengeance. My outlook then becomes being the best version of myself that I can be. When other people observe my life, they will see me full of joy and living a life of success. They see life empowered by a higher power. Life looks different from the mountain tops than from the bottom of a valley. At the bottom, all things look impossible, but at the top, all things are achievable.

Walking is one of my favorite activities. I learned a lot from walking. I am carefree, strong, and unbothered. I hardly think about how my body feels nor the aches and pains, it's just me and nature. It is a time that I am truly at peace and in tune with the environment of the woods. This is how greatness feels, the outside world, and its happenings become harmonious. The discovery of fresh sounds and events are highlighted rather than the negative. The search for greatness should not take a backseat to space and time. Enjoyment in the outcome or searching for greatness becomes the goal. Look at each step as a leap for your soul that will lead to something better than what you have. Do not look at it like a chore, but a spiritual experience that has a topping of whipped cream or a delightful scoop of vanilla ice cream.

The journey of life is full of signs and wonders. There are always miracles waiting to happen. It is really an understatement to say seeking is a lifelong journey because this passes from generation to generation.

> 11 *He has made everything beautiful and appropriate in*
> *its time. He has also planted eternity [a sense of divine*
> *purpose] in the human heart [a mysterious longing*
> *which nothing under the sun can satisfy, except God]*
> *—yet man cannot find out (comprehend, grasp) what*

*God has done (His overall plan) from the beginning to
    the end.*
*12 I know that there is nothing better for them than to
    rejoice and to do good as long as they live;*
*13 and also that every man should eat and drink and see
    and enjoy the good of all his labor—it is the gift
    of God.*
*14 I know that whatever God does, it endures forever;
    nothing can be added to it nor can anything be taken
    from it, for God does it so that men will fear and
    worship Him [with awe-filled reverence, knowing that
    He is God].*

ECCLESIASTES 3:11-14 (AMP)

When we think about a dreamer, the biblical person we can relate to is Joseph. When we look at the natural world for a dreamer, do you relate that story to yourself? Yes, you can look in the mirror and see yourself as a dreamer. Say hello to the dreamer. Every time you allow yourself to be creative, there is a dream waiting to come to life. Articulate that to yourself. There are things that i what you to accomplish and places I want you to see. Embrace what you see in the spiritual mirror and speak it into existence.

When we stop casting aside what we see as just a fleeting thought and consider it to be an action to be taken, we will stir up the dreamer in us. Joseph's dream became a reality when he spoke them into the atmosphere. A dreamer speaks what he sees, and at that moment, reality takes hold and puts a divine demand on his behalf.

What are you speaking about yourself? Good or evil? Are you just saying idle words having no merit, or are you speaking words of life because of the dream? You must understand a dreamer cannot and will not fail. Greatness will not allow failure as an option. Dreamers understand they have the power to rule and reign regardless of any pit, jail, lie, or bondage. Those so-called obstacles cannot stop the plan of God. The dream is God-inspired. Dreamers are winners. Yes, the person in the mirror is you, and you are a winner. Here comes the dreamer, and that dream is yours. Accept this truth and be proud because somewhere in life, you will save a nation.

The spirit of fear, self-doubt, and uncertainty causes us to make excuses for lack of success. The people who were being bullied by Goliath, the giant, astonished David. As a warrior and a fighter who killed a lion and a bear, David was a man after God's heart. David's fearlessness would not allow Goliath to rant and rail accusations against the people of God. The people of God made excuses why they could not put Goliath in his place. As a young man full of faith, confidence, and determination, David comes on the scene asking, "Is there not a cause?" When you understand the cause, you stop making excuses. Excuses defeat the cause. A cause is a principle, aim, or movement. One is prepared to defend and advocate at all costs. The one who has the power to determine the outcome of the situation or event because there is trust in God and oneself. When we reduce our fears and allow faith to emerge, excuses will diminish.

Greatness receives the sacrifices. Excuses reject the sacrifice. In the mind of excuses, nothing or anybody is truly worth of a better life of goodness. There is a peace and calmness when you stop making excuses to fail. God did not create his precious people to fail. The beauty of this is that God gives greatness to the just and unjust. So, let us stop saying we are not worthy of God's best, but realize the promises for you and me to be great.

SACRIFICE AFFIRMATIONS

1. God did not give the Spirit of fear, but power, love, and a sound mind. - 2 Timothy 1:7
2. I can do all things through Christ who strengthens me. - Philippians 4:13
3. I am the head and not the tail. - Deuteronomy 28:13
4. Lean not to your own understanding. - Proverbs 3:5-6
5. I have the mind of Christ. - I Corinthians 2:16
6. All things work together for the good of those who are in Christ Jesus. - Romans 8:28
7. Love never fails. - I Corinthians 13: 4-8

When I started this book, this was something I always wanted to do. I had talked about writing a book for several years. So, an opportunity arose to take a writing class, and I jumped at the chance. Now, remember I did not like English all that well. Writing and all its rules were not my thing. However, I have been told that I am a skilled speaker or orator. During this time, I had also written my book and felt this writing class would give me some more information and help me overcome the deficits I thought I had. Just like any excellent writer, I read the material given for the class hoping to gleam new and important writing techniques. The first batch of material was good, but from some notes I had, I could not retain any information. My heart sank. My thought was, "This is just not going to work," but every day, I would read the old and new material. I was writing things that God said to me during our quiet time. Sometimes, I would write things from past experiences. At other times, my spirit would just lead me to talk about everyday events. I knew God had told me this would be an opportunity for me to complete. So, I stayed in faith.

*Now faith is the confidence in what we hope for and
assurance about what we do not see. This is what the
ancients were commended for. By faith we understand
that the universe was formed at God's command, so
that what is seen was not made out of what was
visible.*

HEBREWS 11:1-3 (NIV)

Well, the writing class opened the door to a book writing group. This is where I really picked up speed. My eyes were opened as I no longer was bound by the conventional book writing assignments. The book writing class allowed me the freedom to write and not worry about the rules. The voice that I was given needed to be told in my own way. My story or truth could not be told by someone else, nor could it be communicated with no type of personal experience. Toward the middle part of my journey, while speaking with my daughter, she was excited to help. My daughter could take my pages and pages of notes that I had all around the house in notebooks, folders, post-it notes and organize them into chapters I had already made. Also, she could help connect the pieces into a collective and cohesive thought while also providing filler and transitions to each topic. This was something that my daughter enjoyed doing—reading books into the wee hours of the morning and writing. So, long story short, when I started this book, everything was not in place. I had to trust what I knew God had said I could do. God is only obligated to provide provision on what He has given. Not that God will not intervene in an area if you are off course. However, there is an ease and peace when things come together, because God has spoken to you in your heart about what to do. The hardest part is the initial step. The first step requires hard work and determination when you are working without a clear-cut path. Your goal is known, but when the steps are not laid out, just staying the course with hard work and dedication will produce results. I started the book and done all I could do in the natural and then the supernatural finished the process for me.

One morning, around 6:30 am, my faithful God gave me battle-tested information. God said to me, "Greatness comes in small gold nuggets, and you have to dig for it." During this time, I was also told to go back and read the writing class notes again. Instead of reading the notes with my natural eyes, I started using my spiritual eyes. God said, "Remember Ruth who gleaned in the field. There was always someone who left a little extra so she would have more than enough." God said, "From this day forth, read the writer's notes from your class through a different lens and see what I have allowed to drop on your behalf. You will have more than enough to write this chapter." He also reminded me how greatness develops in small stages, but there is always enough for us to succeed no matter where we are in the stage of our lives. Greatness comes to find you and promote you to the next level and provides the means to finish the divine work that you and I have been given.

My heart is always to please the Father. So, I went back and re-read the very first material given in the writing class through the lens of greatness, and this is what I discovered. No one can be greater than their level of thinking. Your mind will coincide with the mind of Christ. My greatness was already there, but I had to change my position. "Writing is not for me" was a thought that just vanished. Words and analogies to use for my book just flowed. I could tap into the greatness already given to me. I had greatness all along. I was just not looking at things from the right perspective. Things I needed were provided along the way. Other people in my life were placed there who could help me finish the task. This also stresses the importance of other people in your life that stretch you. This may be friends, family, enemies, oh yeah, even the haters, events that challenge us or make you uncomfortable. These things also contribute to our development of greatness. Our mental and spiritual minds get involved, yet tested.

When my greatness has been tested, it will stand in the eye of the storm.

GREATNESS IS A CITY OF LOVE WHERE I AM A CITIZEN

Have you ever thought about what or how a city is built? Building a city takes a lot of thought and work to construct whether it is big or small. There is a coalition of people willing to work in different phase of the process. The primary focus during the building process is to build for the sake of the people and not the notoriety or status quo. Being a showboat does not serve any one person. When we seek for greatness, we must remember we are servants to the people. Greatness is about serving the people. The next thing you need is land and with room leftover to expand as growth happens. I must make sure my desire for greatness is large enough for others to partake in the plan. I cannot afford to be selfish and self-centered. God is in control of my life. Everybody has a part in building the city. Remember the importance of relationships to increase social interactions. Each citizen of the city has a part to play and their part can never be devalued. In each city, we must not build walls to separate people but to encourage unity. Our lives are linked and form a community.

MY EMPOWERING THOUGHTS FOR BOOK CLUB FOR DISCUSSION

When faith and greatness collide, it causes a combustion that opens the secrets of the Kingdom. Now I can see what God sees, and I can hear what God hears and do what God says I can do.

"Oh yea of Little Faith." What does this truly mean? When I dedicate myself to the task at hand, I am given the help of the Father. Things change. When I think about the dedication of a newborn baby, the purpose is to present back to God what He has given you. But it is also to seal through (dedication) what that child will become in the future. This process or act of faith is so powerful because the child grows and experiences life, good or bad. The parent can revert to the words spoken over the child during the dedication. The whole encounter has distinct memories that can be rehearsed in time of need. When we dedicate ourselves to the vision, it will speak when times of uncertainty and doubt come. Our hope can be found back in the time of dedication of our true self, back to the plan of God.

greatness has a bloodline

WHAT IS the first thing that comes to your mind when I say bloodline? A bloodline is your heritage: parents, grandparents, great grandparents, and so on. It comes from both sides of your family, your mother and father. The desire or the tentacles of a bloodline can run deep if you go back generations. What these tentacles are connected to will determine how you and I interact with greatness. How we perceive greatness determines our hunger and desire to achieve our highest or lowest level based upon the dominate bloodline force. The questions we ask ourselves are: Did our ancestors handle failures, challenges, and situations? Were their words seasoned with love, or did they spew out words of contention? What was their thought pattern? How were things handled so that greatness could or would thrive? What legacy was passed on for the next generation to inherit and build upon?

In our search for greatness, how deep we dig will be determined by what guidelines our ancestors left for us to follow. How detailed is the map? Are there stairs of success to help the next generation continue? Is there so much confusion that our minds are constantly being disturbed by old, meaningless, demonic thoughts or ideals?

GREATNESS IS TIED TO YOUR SELF-ACCEPTANCE

We tied our greatness to our ability to accept who God has made us to be. When we try to change ourselves or fit into the mold of who other people, things or situations dictate will ensure we stay in the same position. This stagnant place will hinder your greatness and the level of your achievements. This can be another moment of confusion in the mind. When this fog is there, you cannot see or appreciate who you are and what you deposit into the earth and others' lives.

Self-acceptance is a powerful relationship with yourself. It can make or break you. This is the moment in your life to stop, look and listen or stop, drop and roll. Whichever one is necessary to get past this choking point is what you decide. This phase of your Greatness Journey can be short-lived or a lifelong road to destruction.

Choose today who you want to be... a person of greatness and all its perks or failure with all its valleys. The question for many people is, "How do I just accept who I am when there are so many other forces speaking to my head?" Tapping into greatness means that I acknowledge I am. See yourself through your child lens. The place where everything is perfect, calm, and exciting. The place where there are no obstacles or weights. Your mind, life, and emotions will have to be steered in greatness. Remembering how you see yourself in your down times will direct your actions.

WHERE DOES MY SELF-ACCEPTANCE LINE UP WITH MY BLOODLINE?

The price paid for the shedding of Jesus's blood was a very heavy one. The debt we owed was paid in full. This blood covers every part of our lives. However, this is a choice whether to accept this free gift. This adoption in this new family is available for us to use. Greatness is the act of traveling from one season of your life to another one. Each hinging off the previous one and so on, much like the building blocks we played with as children. Each block that is placed creates a new challenge. Where do I place the new one? Which direction do I build—sideways or upwards? Sometimes, the process is fast and then it slows down when we are plotting our next block needing to be placed. This process is called seasons. Even when we do not know where it ends or begins, neither is important. God knows the beginning and the end of our journey. Because the process may be uncertain, we get anxious, but the personal progress is certain to promote change and development. This experience is priceless. There is so much to learn and unlearn. This is a lifelong journey having a specific destination. You might have some steps to take along the way. Traveling requires a lot of steps as well. You get gas, eat, take bathroom breaks, change directions, change drivers, fix a flat, check the oil, and clean the windshield. Sometimes, you travel through rain, snow, hail or heat, which are all uncomfortable. Traveling also has traffic jams, a few leg cramps, and a few more stops to make. These steps are making forward progress to the journey. Greatness is the same way. All the steps are necessary. Do not fight the process. The end, the destination, is already known. Challenges can be a sign of progress and not defeat.

STEPPING INTO YOUR TRUE SELF

When I think about stepping, I think about paver stones that lead up to a specific house or apartment. At the end of the pavers is a destination as they serve the purpose of smoothing the way. Greatness seekers are people of purpose even when the purpose is not known. Each step we take in life will direct us to our true self. Each step can reflect what we can be. The uncertainty or baby steps we take release a certain energy fueled by determination. This hones in your faith level. Many people are afraid to take these first steps because of fear. Being off-balance requires steadiness that can only be gained with God's direction. As I take more steps and look closely, I see a clearer reflection of what my true self looks like. If I allow the reflection to become a reality, my life will conform to what I see and not the past images in my head. God has such high regard for you and me. All the good that God is lives inside of us. I must believe in God, but I must believe in myself, too.

I know it's hard to keep stepping when there is an unknown destination.

> *Consider it pure joy, my brothers and sisters, whenever*
> *you face trials of many kinds, because you know that*
> *the testing of your faith produces perseverance.*

JAMES 1:2-3 (NIV)

An unknown destination should be an adventure and not a dread, gloom, or a feeling of despair. Excitement should be the driving force that encourages us to step into the unknown, not shy away from it. When we take what we know and mix it with the unknown, it produces the divine, acceptable revelation of truth. Truth brings freedom. Freedom brings liberation. Liberation brings courage to step in the higher places. This helps to reveal your true self. Without adversity, you never know what you can or cannot do.

An accurate reflection of self-reflection will open your mind to the real you. It will diminish the old image you have of yourself and introduce you to the Greatness that is housed on the inside. The shadows of lessor and the opinions of others will disappear. With each victory, you are feeding the new. The old person's image is being shattered. In the adventure of finding your true self, allow yourself the privilege of stepping into the cracks. In fact, challenge yourself to break the rules of life and live a little. Greatness demands that you do so. The risk and the reward are the same. Do not be deceived by the false analogy of taking a risk. When you obtain success, the feeling is undeniable deliverance. Using the gifts given in your bloodline from God provides:

1. Keeps us from harm. - Psalms 12:1
2. God is always with us. - Deuteronomy 31:8
3. God never forgets us. - Isaiah 49:15-16
4. God has a plan to prosper me. - Jeremiah 29:11-13
5. God rewards us when we love our enemies. - Luke 6:35
6. God keeps us safe while we sleep. - Psalms 4:8
7. Good strengthens us and helps us. - Isaiah 41:10
8. He is our refuge and fortress. - Psalms 91:2
9. God will never leave us or forsake us. - Hebrews 13:5
10. Promises and blessing pass to your children. - Acts 2: 39

God keeps us from unforeseen events in our lives. This does not promise a worry-free or stress-free life. When you know that you have already won, the pressure is off. The fight is not a fair fight. It is a shame that the devil actually thinks he can win!

Navigating the highs and lows of your life requires complete trust in the Word. At each stage of the journey, God knows what we can and cannot handle. The things we perceive as harm have been allowed for us to see God's greatness living inside us. For instance, what we see as a negative circumstance or event is an opposition we can handle. The test to pass is not the challenge, but the trust level we have in God. That is the entire purpose of the test... to increase the trust in the Greatness of God and in yourself.

Greatness comes from challenges. Just like muscles that must be built, our reliance upon our Father God has to be built. Each challenge building upon the last one. God has provided a way to overcome any situation as a gift to His children. The bloodline is dcing what it came to do—provide you with greatness. That Greatness is carried with you wherever you go. It provides help and counsel for the direction needed. Every time we speak with the

Father in our self-talk time, it is reconfirming the original plan God made in the Garden.

Self-talking involves using the Word of God, which brings strength and encouragement in those uncomfortable valleys of our lives. The Word hides us under the stream of the blood which cannot be penetrated by any foe. This love is everlasting and never ends. It follows us into eternity. These blessings do not stop with you and me. The bloodline grants future generations that are born into your natural bloodline the same privilege.

It is very apparent the devil understands his assignment. Seemingly, he never gives up or takes any time off. The hallmark of a good and trusted employee is dedication, putting in over-time and going beyond the norm. A good employee will strategize so he can gain an advantage any way he or she can because their higher pay is at the next level. If this process is truly understood by the Church and the everyday lay person, our divine assignments would be completed faster and more effectively. We must strive to develop a champion's mindset. To win at all costs. To put it all on the line. To keep going no matter what.

WHAT CAN HINDER ME FROM ACHIEVING GREATNESS

There will always be hindrances trying to stop our progress in life. My job is to identify them as quickly as possible and to overthrow them. First, let us define a hindrance. Webster defines this as a delay, snag, inconvenience, obstacle, barrier, restraint, limitation or interruption—to be held back or slowed down, to slow the progress of someone or something. Let us talk about a few of these. There are several things that interrupt like time. Delays in time causes undo worry and stress. Confusion is a slight form of insanity, keeping us in a loop of doing the same thing over and over. So, progress is stopped. When progress is stopped or restraints are placed on our ability to excel, a lot of energy can be expelled. That is why it is important to have a reserve of Word that provides strength during these times. Most of the common hindrances to watch and avoid are listed below.

1. Placing other's opinions above the Word of God.
2. Speaking words of self-doubt.
3. Not having proper tools to complete task.
4. Misinformation.
5. Procrastination.
6. Low expectations of yourself.
7. Greatness is not obtainable or necessary.
8. Obtaining a false sense of success.
9. Greatness requires X amount of dollars.
10. Someone else can do it better than you.

To obtain the level of greatness you know lives on the inside of you, work hard to eliminate hindrances trying to entrap you. Fight with everything that you have available. Find every resource you need to find your greatness. Greatness delivers the best, and only you can give that.

Greater is he that is in you, than he that is in the world.

I JOHN 4:4

There are many winds that blow on you from time to time. The north, south, east, and west winds blow all the time without ceasing. Words have a lot of force and turbulence when used in the wrong way. When used correctly, words can be the strongest thing. For example, Hebrews 1:3 describes God as upholding the world by word of His power. Did you ever notice how hurricanes and tornados have strong winds that cause a lot of destruction? Even more amazing is how some things are completely demolished while a structure less than 20 feet away remains untouched. These are things that seem to defy nature and stand strong. Well, that is who you and I are. The structure unscathed by the winds represents how we, as children of the Most High, have the license to enjoy via our heritage, our ancestry, and bloodline. We can tell any storm to cease to exist and change the direction of the invisible winds blowing in our lives.

The question is, "Can my background handle the pressure?" The pushing and pulling, discomfort, of the storm comes to take away the Word hidden in your heart, mind, and soul. That is the object of the enemy. These challenges are just that—an opportunity to test how rooted you are in your bloodline. This is no failure here. The test is building your faith muscles and your resolve to keep your legal rights to the promises of God. Until you understand this, the situation or event will continue to speak to your words contrary to your inheritance. This is not the time to throw in the towel and quit. This is the time to find the eye of the storm where it is quiet and peaceful. Turbulence is all around you and creating a path of destruction. Get out of the way! This is the place where you can hide and gather your protection, the will of God.

He who dwells in the secret place of the Most High shall remain stable and fixed under the shadow of the Almighty [Whose power no foe can withstand].

PSALMS 91:1

Abide in me, and I in you. As the branch cannot bear fruit by itself, unless it abides in the vine, neither can you, unless you abide in me. I am the vine; you are the branches. Whoever abides in me and I in him, he it is that bears much fruit, for apart from me you can do nothing. If anyone does not abide in me he is thrown away like a branch and withers; and the branches are gathered, thrown into the fire, and burned. If you

*abide in me, and my words abide in you, ask whatever
you wish, and it will be done for you.*

JOHN 15:4-7

This is the key to your greatness. To be great requires staying connected to the power source. There is no other way around this. When you are connected to a power source, you carry the same level of power the original source has. The power or capacity of producing greatness stems from our power source, God's Word abiding in inner-most being. Tests or challenges are to test the amount of Word you believe. Where you are missing, greatness in any aspect of your being is the area needing more muscle. The trials are to test your resolve in what Word you have and to increase that level much like strength training. Once you pass this stage of the journey, the next level begins to passing this to your off-spring.

In the book's making, this chapter was supposed to have other material. At the last moment, computer issues and letters that were supposed to comprise the bulk of this chapter were not done. At the last moment, my daughter could tap into the Word instilled in her as a youth and rewrite that chapter from scratch. As a parent in the ministry, you want a legacy to leave behind, and this is a promise of God given in my bloodline; what I started would continue into the next generation. What started as a seed grew and matured in my daughter, Kathryn. I could convey my thoughts and desires what I wanted to accomplish with this chapter. The promise of God's Word provided my seed with the ability to pick up the mantle and help produce this chapter. Greatness is generational and produces a seed after its own kind. This is the genuine test of any seed—how does it produce itself? No seed dies before maturing and bearing more fruit.

MY EMPOWERING THOUGHTS FOR BOOK CLUB DISCUSSION

The streets do not respect the Greatness in you. As I sit and watch the news about George Floyd, Trayvon Martin, and Breonna Taylor, I am saddened, as these are people in whom greatness was not realized they were not valued for who they were. No matter how much greatness lives in you, the streets will never help define it. The street of our country cannot understand what God has deposited inside of each person. The streets do not know how to process the attitude of greatness. The strength of greatness, the poise of the inner man, is groaning to release itself. However, the birthing room of greatness is not available in the streets. Greatness and the desire for it come from the schoolhouse of the heart that pulls the soulish realm of humanity to not allow a street mentality to dictate whether you succeed or fail. The streets do not respect your bloodline.

when the lion roars

I HAVE SAID that beauty is in the eye of the beholder, which is true. In contrast, greatness goes to the bones. Greatness will attach itself to the thoughts and intent of the heart and go to the substance in the bone's marrow. Greatness cannot be analyzed by the naked eye, but the substance of it hides in the deep valley of your soul or humanity. That is why it is difficult to determine how great a person is or will become. If beauty is in the person's eye who has divine eyesight, then greatness can be gauged the same way. Divine eyesight will amplify and project greatness in 3D. Greatness is only visible in 3D. So, you need a special set of eyes or glasses to get the full effect or depth of greatness. The following scriptures describe more closely what I mean. Compare the two verses below.

1 Corinthians 13:12 (NIV) and (KJV)

> *For now, we see only a reflection as in a mirror, then we*
> *shall see face to face. Now I know in part, then I shall*
> *know fully even as I am fully known. (NIV)*
> *For now, we see through a glass, darkly; but then face to*
> *face: now I know in part; but then shall I know even as*
> *also I am known. (KJV)*

Only when we can see clearly how great we are can we behold what it will take for us to accept this truth and walk in it. Vision is imparted to achieving greatness. The questions to each person are, "How do you see yourself? What lens are you looking through? The lens of other people's opinion, the lens of hurt and disappointment, fear, and trauma? The lens of low self-esteem and failure. How about the lens of I do not care or self-centeredness?" Where you were born or what family you were born into determines your lens as well. A good photographer knows how to adjust and changes lens to get the best picture possible. To behold the Greatness in myself, sometimes I need to adjust the lens through which I see myself in order to get the best vision of myself. To get the full effects of my greatness in different seasons, I may have to change my perception of what I see. This is also true when we look at the lens of others. When I look at myself and others, I see the outside and inside simultaneously. How you consider what is the marrow and bone of yourself and others are. What Greatness is hidden deep on the inside you groaning to break free. Let us research the bone and marrow theory.

Webster's Dictionary defines marrow as the soft spongy-like substance in the bone that produces white and red blood cells and platelets (stem cells). Red marrow produces red blood cells, which produce the healing portion of the cell that can make you sick or well. Webster's dictionary also defines bones as protectors of the various organs of the body, which produce red and white cells stems, stores minerals, provide structure, and support mobility. Greatness causes us to walk into destiny. Your greatness has legs to produce structure in your life. It goes to the weakest areas in the body to stop failure. It protects the vision God has put inside of you. When the sickness of failure tries to talk you out of completing your task, greatness gives you a divine transfusion because it is covered by the blood (red cells) of Jesus.

How you see yourself is the primary focus you should have. The view of yourself determines how you respond to others, challenges, relationships, work environment. It is much like a bank account; self-worth is an account where you can only give what you have. The account is to accumulate your measure of labor that has been produced primarily. How much have you labored to love your own self? What is in the account you can give after all your bills have been paid?

FINDING YOUR ROAR

The lion is the king of the jungle, so they say, and his massive body frame and a distinctive roar are bound to get everybody's attention. It is important to have people's attention because the bigger the audience, the bigger the impact. His massive chest cavity and mane makes him the envy of all other cats. His roar can be heard from up to 5 miles or 8 km. The territory he guards can be up to 260 km or 100 square miles. What a powerful animal, the lion or lioness. But like all creatures God made, there are a few weaknesses. They get frustrated easily and rarely take defeat very well. This is when his roar becomes very distinct, the lion's roar is personal. He/she will roar to intimidate when they are frustrated. When they are defeated, you hear their loudest roar. This is a great lesson for us who are striving for greatness and we feel defeated, frustrated, or intimidated. These are times for us to release our roar. WE should dig deep into our soul, mind, will, emotion, and intellect to form a plan which allowing me to produce a stream of air that stabilizes the vocal cords to produce words of encouragement. Words of life and light, words that challenge every demon in hell, every hindrance, and close every door.

When I refuse to roar, my inner frustration stops me from crossing my bridge call victory. My digging and my strategies are not in vain because I now have a roar that causes my frustrations to become a season of blissfulness. Intimidation and defeat become victory and success. When you understand the purpose of your roar, it will become second nature to you. And defy every challenge, wrong decision, wrong turn, every place of procrastination, and every excuse. They will be met with a resounding roar that says, "I am victory, hear me roar." Allow the power of your greatness to roar. Cry and roar, pray and roar, push past the pain and roar. Listen, you may be miles away from your destination, but if you were to roar, whatever is in your path would know that you are on the way. ROAR, LION, ROAR!!! The greatness in you demands it.

Seeking for greatness creates space for people and you to dream. Everybody likes to have their own space from time to time. This time of distancing yourself from others allows you to dream, reflect, and ponder on things that pop in your mind at unauthorized times. Space is a dimension of height, depth, and width where all things exist and move as defined by Webster's Dictionary.

Or put another way, we also defined it as an area or expanse which is free, available, and unoccupied—a scope and freedom to live, think, and develop in a way that suits you.

When I am free to encounter my own thoughts, it ignites the dreamer in both you and I. Dreams tap into the possibility all things are possible, which triggers greatness. Joseph was a dreamer. His brothers called him a dreamer or greatness. Joseph's brother had a hard time relating to him being over them as a leader, but what greatness does is produce the leader in you. Society has a major problem with leaders who dream. Dreamers do not fit into the mold called normal.

Let us look at the world system of doing things. For example, in business, greatness is determined by your results only. Until a track record of results is achieved, a person's greatness is undervalued. The cream rises to the top, and those are the only ones having anything to contribute and promote. However, this small window will be quantified and measured in profitability. If a profit cannot be seen, then the contribution is minimized. Any means necessary to get to the top is justified by the results, whether it is legal or illegal, moral or immoral. Winning at all costs is celebrated and rewarded. Until your value can be profitable, you will sit at the bottom of the barrel.

However, the spiritual world is totally different. There is a collective body to be considered. Each member is at an equal level and needed for other parts to work. Greatness is measured in how the whole body works in conjunction and is inclusive of all parts of the body functioning at maximum level. One part of the body cannot work without another part. The whole body is the sum of its parts. Also, much like what happens in the natural when a part is not functioning or hurt, the body immediately goes into self-healing itself. For example, when there is a cut in the skin, the blood automatically starts clotting to form a scab to protect the inside from outside containments and heal the outer skin. The body of Christ is the same way. Whatever is missing or not functioning at maximum capacity, greatness rises to protect the body in its healing process and protect itself from outside containments.

Everybody has a leader inside of them. When I seek for greatness, it causes my creative juices to flow and I think, live, and move outside the box. This is what dreaming is all about. I see the investments and figure out a way to make it visible. The dreamer sees more than the natural eyes. It questions what is occurring and says another option is possible. The dreamer says all things are possible and I can do this.

The dreamer is much like the lion and roars that greatness is possible. Therefore, God is the center of my life, so I can behold all that He has for me to do.

WALKING THE TIGHT ROPE

Seeking for greatness will sometimes feel you are walking a narrow line high above the clouds of possibilities. For those of us who have a fear of heights or who have not yet received our greatness wings, searching for greatness will feel like walking a tightrope in Timberland boots. It will feel like you do not have the right shoes that allow your feet to grip the rope for balance and stability. To walk this tightrope of greatness, you must have what the Bible calls hinds' feet. A hind is a female deer that is very agile. She will place her hind feet where her front feet have already stepped. She can climb steep mountains and rocky paths with her hind feet. Female deer are sure-footed animals.

It should be the same way in my seeking experience for greatness. I must be sure-footed and able to walk the tightrope of life, because every step is crucial and fear is not an option. Failure is not an option either. To be in high places does not rock my confidence. In fact, greatness gives me a confidence coming from the desire to excel and fly above the clouds where the sun always shines.

My brothers and sisters, this journey of greatness is a precarious course. There will be time to go forward, time to go backward, time to stand still, and a time to sprint. This timing is all about balance and skill. Skills you have and skills learned along the way from others. One thing I know for sure, this can be a gut-wrenching experience when it seems like there is a void. But each step has purpose. Each human experience is surrounded by an invisible and spiritual force that makes tight-rope walking easy. There will be times when your success will not help just yourself, but will advance others. So, know you must always advance forward.

Have I not commanded you? Be strong and courageous.
Do not be afraid; do not be discouraged, for the Lord
your God will be with you wherever you go.

JOSHUA 1:9 (NIV)

He gives strength to the weary and increases the power of
the weak.

ISAIAH 40:29 (NIV)

As I seek for greatness, the very essence of who I am is tied to my ability to discover what is really lacking in my roar. I am in a fight for my life. My mind, will, emotion, and intellect of what makes me human and what makes me spiritual. The two are fused together. The natural collides with the supernatural.

what is mankind that you are mindful of them, human
beings that you care for them? You have made them a
little lower than the angels and crowned them with
glory and honor. You made them rulers over the works
of your hands; you put everything under their[e] feet:
all flocks and herds, and the animals of the wild, the
birds in the sky, and the fish in the sea, all that swim
the paths of the seas.

PSALMS 8:4-8 (NIV)

This all boils down to what value you place on yourself. Searching for greatness will help you stop depreciating yourself and will continually push you to a place of great value and worth. When you are a young man or woman, you are at the pentacle of life's possibilities. That is why something or someone is always trying to disturb your quality of life by making greatness seem an impossible task. This is really the time to find your roar. This cannot be achieved without God.

MY EMPOWERING THOUGHTS FOR BOOK CLUB DISCUSSION

When you seek for greatness, let it become a personal endeavor. Everything out of character should frustrate you to no end. When the lion in frustrated, it is because he cannot capture the prey. The other reason for the aggravation is because things are not going his way. His roar is so loud and personal that everything and every animal take notice. Whatever every other animal is doing comes to a halt. Quickly, the frustration of not being in sync with your vision and dream should make your roar personal. You and I must become comfortable with our DNA, greatness. Greatness completes a full circle in your life toward developing the roar unique to you. That means just being average is elevated to the supernatural. Your Greatness is a treasure waiting for you to discover the vast riches it has in store for you. You have the map and all you need to do now is follow it!

the dance

REMEMBER WHEN YOU WERE A CHILD, and it was time for your birthday or Christmas Eve? Waiting for that day was so exciting that you could not contain your emotions. Months and days before your birthday, you would count down how many days were left before your birthday. Waiting for Christmas was the count-down month, with 24 days before the arrival of Santa. Each day brought a new level of excitement. You would daydream about what gift you might receive. Every other day dropping hints to your relatives and friends about what you really wanted. You kept envisioning in your head if the gifts you were going to receive were the ones you had asked for or was there going to be something different and special. Oh, the endless possibilities!

When you talked to your friends or anybody who would listen, there was a high pitch to your voice and a long story to tell, detail by detail, if the present was a bike, it was the fastest bike in the world. If the present was a doll, it was the prettiest doll ever, with long hair and dressed to kill (figure of speech). If it was a new pair of shoes or a coat, the shoes made you run faster and the coat was the warmest ever. The excitement was so contagious you could draw a crowd in just a few minutes. There were stories we swapped with each other, much like stories men tell in the barbershop with the twinkle in your eye and the smile on your face. The hand movements helped describe every detail of the future event sure to come. Your feet shuffled like you were at a school dance. Your body swayed with each moment that had stopped long enough to embrace the contagious excitement. The level of anticipation filled time and seemed like an eternity waiting on the story's conclusion. However, this small moment in time waiting for Christmas brought an awareness of just how slow time could be. By the time you finished telling your story of future bliss, everyone around you was just as excited as you were. The most annoying thing was there were no gifts and no Santa. Only a mental picture that had been painted on the canvas of your mind through a simple act called excitement. This exciting conversation and the future ones you will have made non-believers now became true believers. Anticipation had put a roof over a dream and now there was a group of drooling people lock in to an event that has not occurred only talked about. There was a group that had been moved to tears of joy, hope beyond all measure, just because someone had gotten excited about an event that has not yet happened. There they stand, eye wide, ears pointed, hearts racing and drool, now this is excitement to the tenth power.

Gifts that had not been opened and dreams not yet fulfilled, your conversation had the hope of wanting to manifest itself where others dare not tread. An unconditional love to overcome all obstacles would dare raise its head to anything less to accomplish was never a thought that entered the child's mind. This was not even a possibility or outcome because of a simple emotion called excitement.

So, it is with our seeking for Greatness, the excitement about the experience should always draw a crowd. This should be a day-to-day journey of anticipation of what is ahead and the prize waiting for you. It should always keep a light in your eyes and a smile on your face. Your feet moving forward as you dance with the winds of life that blow you here, there, and everywhere. Also, when you open your mouth, a drool should be visible. The excitement should move you to tears and joy. Even though the end has not been obtained, the dream should be rehearsed and expected as a day of excitement and success. Each day the journey is unfolding creates a joy. This is the good life that is the engine that drives your search for greatness. Searching for greatness that lies in the cornfield of life waiting to be harvested.

Search for greatness is like having a dance with yourself and creating a dance move that will work with your expression of dance. Some days it feels like hip-hop. The next day it might be ballroom dancing, and another day it will be a good slow dance. The rhythm of your experiences in life will determine the type of dance. Each dance is different but necessary to release the pressures and stresses of your life, but has a purpose like the joy and fulfillment of success. Greatness wants to dance with you and me. Make sure you dress for the dance.

I remember going to dances as a young girl and the anticipation of going to the event. The anticipation of going was the beginning highlights. The first question was who else was going to dance? Which one of my friends was going? These were important questions because Certain people brought laughter, certain people brought a new dance move, and certain people brought drama and chaos to be avoided at all cost. The next important question was the date, time, and place. Arrangements had to be made, and schedules had to be adjusted. At some point, who was throwing the party and who had invited who was the next hurdle to overcome? Did someone invite you? Preferably, a boy had asked if you were going to be there or a close home girl. Last but not least, what were you wearing and how were you going to fix your hair? What you were wearing, the granddaddy question of them all. All these questions needed an answer if you were going to the dance.

Well, in my search or seeking for greatness, I had to ask some of the same questions.

1. Am I going to the dance?
2. Is there a date, time, or place?
3. Who is going with me?
4. What will I wear?
5. Who will take me there?
6. Who will pick me up after the dance?

In my heart, the main purpose of the dance is to have fun. There may be many other objections occurring—some planned and some unplanned. The primary objective is to have fun and so, with the journey of greatness, have fun, but know that other obstacles might occur. Fun is the objective of your search for greatness. If this is not established, somewhere along the way, the dance with greatness will be quite boring. As I write this book, I tell myself to have fun writing each day, as it is a new dance.

Writing a book is a process, but also a dance. This book about greatness is a by-product of love from the Father. If love could talk, what would it say?

Good evening, I am love. What is your name? It is a pleasure to meet you. I heard we have a lot in common. So, let's share some of our commonalities. I always look to the heart and not the outside appearance. I am not concerned about your clothes, but I like you. I am drawn to your intent and purpose. I understand you have been mistreated from time to time, but like me, forgiveness is your strongest asset. Times of reflection are important to me. So learn to look through the mirror of life and not others' opinion. I sometimes hide behind the mask of shyness or being timid, but really, I am strong. In fact, I do not bow down to any weakness. There are many who use me for all the wrong reasons, but I always shatter their shallow thoughts and images because love is kind and perfect. Love goes down into the marrow and bones to expose what the real deal is. You may think you are using me, but really, I am using you. Simply because love never fails. My assignment will always be complete. That is the way love is. I love you.

To see love, just push back the curtain. Love is always standing there. Love is multi-faceted, but still functions in unison despite its many kinds. Love stands in our presence, waiting for humanity to embrace it. Love functions have not been tapped into as you and I are still searching. This is the dance.

YOU CAN NOT LIVE WITHOUT ME

How connected are you to God? This connection is a complex and elaborate part of the dance. In order to connect with God, there are ways to do so in a meaningful and powerful way. Just like the dance, everyone has their own expression and interpretation of how the music feels to them. This expression is neither right nor wrong, just personal. The music of your life experience sets your personal dance. Sometimes, the whole dance is determined by the mood of the music. The music has highs and lows that evoke an inner emotion personal to you. Maybe you like the beat, maybe the lyrics, maybe the words remind you of a past event or a splendid memory and yet the opposite can be true as well. Sometimes, the music of our lives may stir up bad or negative emotions. Whatever the feeling, searching for the right music determines how you sway. As the young people say, it is about swag. The music of greatness in your dance with God should be personal to you and connect you to Him. How to accomplish this is provided in some suggestions I have listed below.

HOW TO CONNECT WITH GOD

1. Slow down.
2. Meditate or pray.
3. Enjoy the journey and its process.
4. Stay open to finding God in yourself.
5. Look for God in every person you meet.
6. Stay open to find God in expected places.
7. Find music that touches your soul.
8. Honor your body, family, or friends.

To connect to God, I must feel his presence enough to trust him with my life. This trust is much, so a part of my everyday life it requires humility. Humility is a position and place where I submit to Him my entire will, emotion, and intellect. I yield to Him at all costs. Nothing else matters or comes before that trust, even my own desires, thoughts, and will. This position I place myself in will challenge my very being. Because God is everything or nothing, but I must decide that within myself. This decision will be your own sacrifice because it is the dance of love.

I must learn to follow and not try to lead with my dance partner. I understand how I am connected, even though I am my own individual person. This comes through my prayers, my study time, and meditation, which are centered on who He is and who I am in Him. I fused myself into the identity of Him. I am connected through my relationship with my husband, friends, grandchildren, and family. I connect through kindness and constant devotion to them. God's wisdom is critical to my connections to Him and those around me. I am learning how to understand His creative ability, His desires, His love, and His passion. This is the dance that I must learn and follow the pattern of Christ. All dances have a certain set of steps that are unique. Once you learn the dance, then you can teach it to others.

You may ask, "What about the people who can't dance?" Remember, the dance expresses your innermost being. This may take work, and you might not dance like anybody else. However, there is a dance within you. It is like being at home by yourself and turning the music to ten and dancing with all your might. Nobody cares if you are on the beat or what it looks like. Your dance is just a response to how the music makes you feel on the inside. It is a surge of emotions that produce movement in your body. Your favorite song will not allow you to just sit still; you move in response to it. What or how you move is an involuntary action. You cannot stop it. The dance never ends, as it is a work in progress. When I am connected, my spiritual well-being is enhanced and becomes more intense. Greatness causes you to connect to God and search inwardly. Connection to someone else or something else causes you to connect outwardly. This is the difference in the dance.

Positive experiences in my life do not define the current moment; they define where I am going in the future. The opposite is true as well. This experience you have dictates where you are going, therefore, be on guard what you allow in your personal sphere. Make sure you have the right dance partner you can follow. Otherwise, you will be led astray from the Greatness you hope to achieve. To get to my future, there will always be events trying to define a moment. Moments are just glitches in time that try to alter the future events of your life. Greatness pushes past moments in time and sees what is going on in relation to the end purpose of your life. Greatness choreographs steps and gives impromptu changes as it redirects you back to your assigned path or journey.

THE TWO-STEP VERSUS PRAISE DANCE

We can hinge greatness between where you were and where you are now. It is called the dance of life. The dance may start off with just a few steps, sometimes unsure and baby steps. There will eventually come a time when your legs get stronger and you will be more sure-footed about learning the dance of life, but we all start somewhere. Who you are and what you bring to the table starts in a crazy, out-of-step phase, but this is unique to you and will feel normal with age and experience.

This is where you will begin to two-step. The two-step is a simple but beautiful dance. Just only a short while ago, you could barely make one step at a time, much less multiple steps in time to music. The two-step provides a powerful, fulfilling, and amazing gear to start your motor running. This sets you up for the final and profound journey that is just around the corner. You are in motion. You are not looking back at how it started; you are focusing on where you are now doing the two-step. Watch out now! You are stepping your way into quick and precise steps.

As you move in sync with the beat of your Greatness journey, you will float without a care in the world knowing with great assurance the challenges in life are trying to hold you hostage. No looking back, as it will cost you the race. The challenges in life steer your feet in another path, but if you tap into the praise dance, this phase is not a problem. Moving forward in your dance of life allows you to make choices and not end up in an undesirable situation or circumstance. How you dance along the way will surely determine where you land. The praise dance conveys a language that turns into notes, lyrics, and rhythms not understood by anyone else but you and God. You take out of a state of being vulnerable and expose you to a state of the supernatural.

What is unique about the praise dance is that is not choreographed. It comes from the heart and flows from a divine place. Only you can translate what it means. This type of dance affects the heart and mind. You can see it and embrace it. It is your truth speaking on your behalf. Praise dance is a message inside a message that the composer, God, can only understand. The dance is a response to the Creator. Praise dancing involves the use of all the outward expression of your being. Your total being comprises arms, legs, eyes, hands, feet, and ears working in divine unity to express greatness.

The Greater you and I is like a dance that is always looking for the newest music, the newest steps, and the enjoyment of learning how to express what we find. Remember from Chapter 7, the subject was bloodline. Here is where my other daughter, Ebony, comes on the screen. Greatness has blessed me in that my seed for greatness in Him is passed to the next generation. Ebony is the total of my seed of praise and worship. With little formal training, she has to ability to dance and express God's love in dance. Ebony reaches on the inside of herself and expresses visually what God is saying to an outside audience. Praise and worship is the dance of love between you and God. How you dance in response to God is your dance. Move your hands. Move your feet. Move your head. Move your arms. Move your legs. Get on the dance floor and tear it up!

MY EMPOWERING THOUGHTS FOR BOOK CLUB DISCUSSION

My biggest challenge is learning how to commit to the relationship of greatness and not just on an emotional train ride. Relationships can be hard to develop. Some are very disappointing. The great ones that last only come from total and genuine commitment. Giving of one's self is difficult. There are so many blind spots having oil slick that makes is easy to fall apart. Commitment is a very intimidating word, but the act itself can be quite fulfilling. The question is, what are you willing to give up to make things work? What are you holding onto that is hindering the relationship? What are you looking to get from the relationship? Committing to the lifestyle of greatness is the very first step. You acknowledge you are on a greatness journey. When this happens, the other steps necessary for success fall into place. Life lessons can be painful, but we are all learning how to operate under pressure and push through the pain. There will be day-to-day challenges that come. At the end of each day, there is always a time of rest. God himself will refresh your body, mind, and Spirit because tomorrow is a new day.

you can make it – the destination is in view

AS WE STRIVE to move forward, the one thing that brings us peace is our accomplishments. Good success does not involve or measure the level of greatness you are currently in. What matters more than anything is the forward motion. The forward motion brings a level of peace and contentment.

> *Submit to God and be at peace with him, in this way*
> *prosperity will come to you. Accept instruction from*
> *his mouth and lay up his words in your hearts.*

JOB 22:21-22 (NIV)

When I follow my heart's destiny, my feet will always be on solid ground. That solid ground is the path to the greatness for which I am searching. Any accomplishment brings a manifestation of peace and confidence. When we are confident, all things are possible, courage and strength will stop at nothing, and a dream becomes a reality in that moment—not in the future. My forward motion demands possibilities and opportunities to appear where there were none. The enemy's job is to get in a position of stale-mate. A moving target is much harder to hit than one standing still. Forward motion eliminates times in my life which can lead to stagnation. Pushing forward with a purpose in mind will be the one tool that you must develop.

I CAN MAKE IT

"Can" and "may" are just some three-letter words. However, the word can carry with it a lot of power and authority. "Can" is a word introduced early into our vocabulary and spelled in kindergarten. Let's define this easy speaking word most of us learned before we went to school. The word means to do, to be permitted, to do; to have the ability, awareness of impossibility and possibility, or an opportunity. The word "may" is more polite. The word "may" is used in formal situations. The biblical definition of the word "can" means this: to know, to have sufficient strength or physical power, to be possible, to have moral power; to have requisite knowledge, experience or skill and to overcome obstacles.

God wants His people to have an "I can do" attitude about whatever we do for Him and through Him.

> The workers labored faithfully. Over them to direct them were Jahath and Obadiah, Levites descended from Merari, and Zechariah and Meshullam, descended from Kohath. The Levites – all who were skilled in playing musical instruments- had charge of the laborers and supervised all the workers from job to job. Some of the Levites were secretaries, scribes and gatekeepers.
>
> 2 CHRONICLES 34:12-13 (NIV)

And David shepherded them with integrity of heart, with skillful hands he led them.

PSALMS 78:72 (NIV)

Do you see someone skilled in their work? They will serve before kings, they will not serve before officials of low rank.

PROVERBS 22:29 (NIV)

So Bezalel, Oholiab and every skilled person to whom the Lord has given skill and ability to know how to carry out all the work of constructing the sanctuary are to do the work just as the Lord has commanded.

EXODUS 36:1

Whatever I have, where I am, I can make it through anything abiding in the One who makes me who I am. When I say I can, I am saying My Father has put enough power, wisdom, understanding, and knowledge in me and no matter what, I can overcome. Because of what God has put inside of me, nothing can stop me. Most people do not really know what is inside of them. Indulge this thought for a minute.

Therefore, we do not lose heart. Though outwardly we are wasting away, yet inwardly we are being renewed day by day. For our light and momentary troubles are achieving for us an eternal glory that far outweighs them all. So, we fix our eyes not on what is seen, but on what is unseen, since what is seen is temporary, but what is unseen is eternal.

2 CORINTHIANS 4:16-18

The spirit [conscience] of man is the lamp of the Lord, searching and examining all the inner most parts of his being.

PROVERBS 20:27

Greatness is the companion of "I can." When I realize I can, the Spirit or desire for greatness takes over and directs me from impossibilities to possibilities. "I can" heightens my desire for more knowledge or assurance. When fresh adventures surface, this opens new ideas, strategies, and solutions. Greatness is not always visible. It requires thinking beyond the normal capacity. When we seek God, He gives us thoughts to help us achieve our greatness.

THE GOOD LIFE

When we discover how much we love being who we are and accept our strengths and weakness, we will begin what we know as the Good Life. When I appreciate my strengths, the weakness pales in comparison. I see the weakness, but they no longer considered my identity as it does not line-up with the Word of God. My weakness is perfected with the new belief that I have God working through me and not who I am not. You are good at what you do. Do not be afraid to show your knowledge and wisdom as it is giving glory to God the

Father. The Good Life should be Heaven on earth, literally. God's glory should shine and cannot be covered or hid. How else is God's greatness to be shown except through you? However, balance greatness with humility and consideration of others. When you truly tap into your greatness, it demands respect. Greatness and authority open the door to the Good Life when it's given to others. There is no envy or jealousy, strife or devaluation of others when I possess my greatness.

> And Jesus replied to him, "You shall love the Lord your God with all your heart, and with all your soul, and will all your mind. This is the first commandment and greatest commandment. The second is like it, "You shall love your neighbor as yourself [that is, unselfishly seek the best or higher good for others]. The whole Law and the [writings of the] Prophets depend upon these two commandments.
>
> MATTHEW 22:37-40 (AMP)

My moral greatness encourages character to rise and surface, which triggers excellence in myself and others. This is the most overlooked aspect of greatness. Greatness wishes others to be on the same level. The equalizer on the levels of greatness is love. Loving others on the same level as myself is the deeper level. This shouts to everyone I have arrived at the place where God originally wanted for all people. Greatness does not belong to a specific person, group, family or church members. The greatness extends God's love to me. Love is expected and required for me to think and act the same way to others. The relationship denotes an equal sign between my earthly relationships as the true level of my greatness in God. A relationship with people exists in tandem with the relationship I share with God. The two are fused together.

If anyone says, "I love God," and hates [works against] his [Christian] brother he is a liar; for the one who does not love his brother whom he has seen, cannot love God whom he has not seen.

1 JOHN 4:20

Both spiritual laws usher you into the Good Life. This should be built on your quest for greatness. When someone is living the "good life," it is not just the natural possession, even though they will manifest automatically; the whole well-being of your inner man will be involved as well. Not just being a good person, but having a well "being" living on the inside of you. Anybody can be a good person. However, the wellness of your being flow outward. Love is the center of all things, and anything lacking love cannot be well.

Beloved, I wish above all things that thou mayest prosper and be in health, even as they soul prospereth.

3 JOHN 2

The word "even" here denotes a balance of the three things: health in any area of the physical body or the inner man (well-being) and the ability to prosper. The parts are interrelated and interchangeable. You cannot have one without the other. So, if one part is not doing well, then it must be balanced out with the other parts. There is no way around this verse and no other way to achieve the balance without following the Spiritual Law. Therefore, someone who is loyal, honest, trustworthy, giving, and kind is full of principles of greatness. Covetousness, being selfish, gossiping, and mistreating others are hindrances to greatness. Greatness allows us to cover every base in life so we are led to home base; we will not get tagged out.

MY EMPOWERING THOUGHTS FOR BOOK DISCUSSION

My destination is in view on this greatness journey. This is only one direction, and it is forward. We learn from life that looking back can cost you everything. It would be an excellent suggestion to take away the rear window, and the side mirrors, too. These things can keep up looking backward from time to time. These items may be necessary when you are driving a vehicle, but for life's journey, they can be a hindrance. Notice I use the words "can be." The Greatness journey should be so exciting that the desire to look back does not become an option. There is more in front of you to experience than what is behind you... Behold your future it GREATER than your past. You have a front-seat view of your future. What do you see? Greatness!

acknowledgments

BISHOP FREDRICK M. BROWN

Discovering your greatness is one of the most vital but often overlooked aspects of the human life. Its discovery is the difference between those who experience success or failure, happiness or sadness, and moving from average to being super achievers. Earline Neal has spent years teaching individuals how to tap into innate human treasures God has placed in them. This book will further assist in that objective and cause a lifetime of success in the lives of those who read it.

SISTER JEAN ENGLISH

Earline has worn many mantles throughout our thirty-plus years of friendship: singer, dancer, choreographer, instructor, adult advisor, prayer warrior, teacher, preacher, mother, wife, and now, an author. Our extraordinary relationship in Christ has lasted for over thirty years. Within that time, I have always known her to be a true and faithful friend. She has always been a woman of purpose, dedicated to duty, and a seeker of *wisdom (a Kingdom Woman)*.

I recall one story about her purpose as a prayer warrior. Over 30 years ago, as members at Outreach for Christ Christian Center, three sisters in Christ formed a prayer circle consisting of Chiquitta Cheese, Earline, and me (Jean English). We wrote out our prayer requests. Chiquitta requested prayer for her family explicitly in raising her son. I wanted to finish University and get a job with the school system because I was raising three sons. Earline's prayer request was *wisdom*.

We prayed earnestly for each other's requests. Chiquitta raised her son to be a fine young man who became a musically talented Man of God. After years of hard work, I received my Masters+ in School Counseling. Earline has received *wisdom* from God. Requesting *wisdom* may have seemed like a small prayer request, but the value returned has been priceless. James 1:5 (NIV) says, "If any of you lacks wisdom, you should ask of God, who gives generously to all without finding fault, and it will be given to you." Out of her many accolades and accomplishments, *wisdom* has been the greatest gift received.